TRACKING THE WILD WOMAN ARCHETYPE

by
STACEY SHELBY

CHIRON PUBLICATIONS • ASHEVILLE, NORTH CAROLINA

www.ChironPublications.com

Interior and cover design by Danijela Mijailović
Printed primarily in the United States of America.

ISBN 978-1-63051-484-6 paperback
ISBN 978-1-63051-485-3 hardcover
ISBN 978-1-63051-486-0 electronic
ISBN 978-1-63051-487-7 limited edition paperback

Library of Congress Cataloging-in-Publication Data

Names: Shelby, Stacey, author.
Title: Tracking the wild woman archetype / by Stacey Shelby.
Description: Asheville, North Carolina : Chiron Publications, [2018] |
    Includes bibliographical references and index.
Identifiers: LCCN 2017059325| ISBN 9781630514846 (pbk. : alk. paper) |
    ISBN 9781630514853 (hardcover : alk. paper)
Subjects: LCSH: Wild women. | Archetype (Psychology) | Individuation
    (Psychology) | Women--Sexual behavior. | Alchemy.
Classification: LCC GN372 .S525 2018 | DDC 306.7082--dc23
LC record available at https://lccn.loc.gov/2017059325

Dedications and Acknowledgments

Several people contributed to this book and my personal process; I am deeply changed and grateful. Foremost, I want to acknowledge my son, Asher, who inspires me to be a woman of depth and reach—"a big fat mama tree." Such grounding helps me grow both downward and upward. As well, I am appreciative to the wild woman and her entourage for tracking me from the beginning of this project.

Table of Contents

INTRODUCTION
The Rich Soil

Many fabulous works were studied to inform this book, which originally began as my doctoral research in the field of depth psychology; I specialized in Jungian and archetypal psychology at Pacifica Graduate Institute in Carpinteria, California. Pacifica provided the fertile soil where this book was first seeded; it is a unique school dedicated to tending the *anima mundi*, the world's soul. So too is this book. The question guiding this journey is: What are some of the ways a woman who has recovered the wild woman archetype expresses her sexuality and engages in relationships? The telos of this book is to explore how a woman who has reclaimed the wild woman archetype—who is individuating and differentiating from culture—can navigate the paradox of autonomy and togetherness and how this is expressed sexually and in relationships.

To weave our way to answers are four sections or juicy categories called: the Wild Woman Archetype, which focuses on the definition of that archetype and invokes it; Women's Psychological Development; Relationship; and Sexuality, as expressed by women who are conscious of the wild woman within. There is much literature on female sexuality and relationship, but not much that is specific to a woman who has been individuating and reclaiming the wild woman archetype; it is that gap that this work fills.

This work uses the research methodology of alchemical hermeneutics described in *The Wounded Researcher: Research with Soul in Mind* by Robert Romanyshyn (2007). It is an unconventional methodology not readily found in traditional academic institutions, and it acknowledges that researchers are often called to their work through personal wounding and complexes. This research methodology is an alchemical process that affects the researcher. This research deeply affected me as I leaned into the questions around sexuality and relationship. Part of the alchemical hermeneutic process involves dialogue with the psyche through dreams, imagination, and synchronicities throughout. The process also includes reading the *text* of significant, lived relationships in order to ground the research in praxis. Interpersonal relationship can be considered a text because it is a symbolic manifestation of the workings of the autonomous psyche. Ultimately, inside and outside are reflections of each other, and a relationship is comparable to a work of art (and vice versa) and is therefore valid as text. I hope that by sharing my research, experience, and authentic expression, other women will recognize and question their own existing paradigms and find their own unique expressions.

CHAPTER 1
The Base Metal

Spring

Somewhere
  a black bear
    has just risen from sleep
     and is staring

down the mountain.
  All night
    in the brisk and shallow restlessness
     of early spring

I think of her,
  her four black fists
    flicking the gravel,
     her tongue

like a red fire
  touching the grass,
    the cold water.
     There is only one question:

how to love this world.
  I think of her
    rising
     like a black and leafy ledge

to sharpen her claws against
  the silence
    of the trees.
     Whatever else

my life is
  with its poems
    and its music
     and its glass cities,

it is also this dazzling darkness
  coming
    down the mountain,
     breathing and tasting;

all day I think of her—
  her white teeth,
    her wordlessness,
     her perfect love.

—Mary Oliver, 1983, p. 45

Coexist with Bears

I live in a community that has a lot of bears, and there are signs around town that promote ideas like "coexist with bears" and "conservation through coexistence." I love those symbols of living with the wild woman. Living with bears requires respect for them, awareness of them, and knowledge of them. Living with the wild woman archetype requires the same.

Let us gather our provisions and begin tracking the wild woman so that we can get to know her, describe her to others, interpret her movements, and form a relationship with her. We are looking for her tracks that have been padded down methodically for eons. We are looking for the archetype of the wild woman. While each of us has a unique karmic destiny, there are also commonalities based on our sharing of Western culture, which has contributed to the wounding of many women. In this initial chapter, I offer a glimpse of my personal work and hope you will find your own resonance with it.

First, let us create some common language by attempting preliminary definitions of difficult concepts. An archetype is an energetic force that is preexistent and predetermined. As an analogy, an acorn inheres to an oak, just as the wild woman archetype is innate to women. The imprint of archetypal energy is relatively stable and predictable; it is the first or original (*arkhe*) pattern, model, or type (*typos*). Archetypes are *a priori* instinct types, which provide the occasion and pattern for our activities insofar as we function instinctively. The wild woman archetype is the first pattern of a woman—before culturalization or exposure to society. Although it has been around forever, the wild woman was named and brought out of shadow by Clarissa Pinkola Estés (1992) in her book *Women Who Run with the Wolves: Myths and Stories of the Wild Woman Archetype*. It is difficult to define something so mysterious, but we can think of this archetype as nothing less than the innate instinctual Self and also as the personification of the natural instinctive psyche. We will continue the development of our definition of the wild woman as we go along.

Another important definition is patriarchy. This is a social system in which males hold the dominant power and authority as applied to government, moral code, and family, wherein father figures rule. The modern-day Western world originated with a patriarchal system. Both Christianity and ancient Greek culture, the systems that form the foundation of current Western culture and society, privileged males. As such, we see the world and ourselves through a patriarchal lens, at least until we become conscious of that lens. The patriarchal lens favors masculine values over the more subtle and mysterious feminine values. Western culture has become far out of balance with patriarchal dominance, and even though there is backlash, the patriarchal model continues to hold dominion—and it is holding on tight as we witness far-right conservatism in the United States.

A wild woman is someone who has become conscious of some of the ways culture has over-domesticated her: she has become aware of her own wild, instinctual, animal nature. Many women within patriarchies are socialized in a way that leads them to be overly *civilized* or overly *domesticated* from birth, and that domestication affects how they express their sexuality and engage in relationships. When women become conscious of the wild woman archetype, they become free to explore sexuality and relationships on their own terms. The wild woman captures the essence of rebelling against righteous sexual values and the over-domestication of women.

That essential wildness brings to mind the frequently noted archetype of the *bad boy* or the *wild child* who rebels against an overly one-sided, patriarchal society. In the compensatory role of the eternal boy—in Latin, *puer*—rebelliousness against the domination of a father's values brings balance. In a generative role, the bad boy who is not behaving nicely counterbalances the dominant culture and brings in new ideas that disturb existing structures.

A woman accessing the generative wild child girl or bad girl—in Latin, *puella*—can retain spunk, spontaneity, and playfulness in her life. It is this generative *puella* with whom we may want to foster a relationship by integrating some of our own rebelliousness. We do not as often hear of the bad girl (unless it is referring to promiscuity) who rebels against overly one-sided patriarchal values and also against an overly conservative matrilineage. It is usually the matrilineage that teaches girls that it is best to not have sexual relations with a male unless he is committed to a long-term, heterosexual (of course), monogamous relationship. "Why would he buy the cow if he is getting the milk for free?" We can unconsciously absorb the messages that girls were to be seen and not heard and to keep our mouths—and legs—closed. Those were virtuous precepts and would secure a long-term husband who would be faithful and a provider. These are from the voices of the ghosts in our psyches who haunt us.

With the exception of the man who became my husband and the father of my child (later becoming my ex-husband and then, eventually, my friend), I was—and am—usually attracted to the "bad-boy" types. Although they can bring counterbalance to the patriarchy, those relationships were often characterized by casual sex and were usually short-term. Such relationships can create feelings of shame for our sexuality, desires, passions, and yearnings. The short-term gratification can be exhilarating and bring sweetness, after he has flown off we can feel unworthy of love or weak because we gave in to our desires and attractions. Fortunately, many women, including me, have long-term girlfriends who get it, and as part of the sisterhood, we soothe and love each other anyway. Knowing we are not alone in this pain makes it more bearable.

The Wild Virgin to The Wild Woman

I began my research with what I called the *wild virgin* archetype, defining *virgin* the way Esther Harding (1971) did: as referring to a self-possessed woman who was "one-in-herself" (p. 79). Then came a dream that had three parts.

First, I was talking to a bone-weary restaurateur, who was in service to certain old, sleepless ghosts that occupied his restaurant at night; I asked him what he did that made him happy. (Nothing. He served those old ghosts.) Second, he drove me to my new therapist, Nikki (a dream-world therapist), a woman who lived outside of cultural values and in integrity to her deeper self; she was rather unorthodox, sexually liberal, and nonjudgmental—a wild rebel woman. She saw clients at night and was comfortable with night creatures (there was a bat in her office). In the third part, I was with a man whom I loved and wanted to unite with sexually, but the old ghosts of the past kept following us around, shaming us, and preventing our union.

This dream came while I was reading about the *mysterium coniunctionis* (mysterious conjunction) in alchemy. These old, puritanical ghosts were preventing me from uniting with the masculine (on both the inner and external levels). It began to feel as if moving toward the *virginal* in the puritanical and chaste sense, as well as in the sovereign, "I don't need a man" sense was a defense against vulnerability. I was moving toward my core wound—and to my call to what became this book.

I come from a lineage of women who had been in unhappy marriages with men who were violent, alcoholic, sexually roaming, and controlling. These feisty, beautiful women were unable to leave their marriages because they did not have the resources to do so. They were trapped. When I was in my twenties, my mother gave me $2,000 and said, "Keep it hidden away from your man, and use it to get out if you ever need to." The money had come from a small legacy my grandmother left to her five living children. My mother told me my grandmother could not leave my grandfather. My Nana appears in my dreams often. She was a beautiful, spunky young woman who liked to write poetry and have fun, and she was also able to see those who had crossed over to the other side—in particular, her youngest son. As a young woman, she fell in love with my grandfather, who grew into a miserable, violent man and who was not very well-liked—never mind well-loved. I think he remained a wounded boy in search of his absent mother his whole life and never grew up into a mature man.

The times and inner messages changed from 1970. Many women now have careers and contribute to the household income, but it is rare that a woman earns more than her husband; men are still the primary breadwinners. Of course, courageous women had been cutting the path prior to 1970, but my worldview was largely unaffected by the progress of women's liberation. If I navigated with propriety, we could be part of the white-picket-fence club: married, two-and-a-half children (the statistical average, but two would be fine), a dog, a house with the proverbial white picket fence, and of course a faithful, happy husband who would provide for us. That was equivalent to happiness or, more accurately, security and completeness.

Many of us creative women are gifted at turning envisioned ideas into reality. I was asleep in the dream of the culture, and it was lulling me into deeper slumber so that, by my early 30s, I had created the white-picket-fence dream. I could even shake up a fabulous crantini at our Saturday night house parties. But that did not make me feel whole—at all. The lacuna in me widened until I felt only a gaping wound. By the time I was 38, my husband and I had separated, which forced me to begin waking up. I was lost as I entered the second half of my life, the phase upon which Jung placed so much emphasis. I was disillusioned and let go, as Christine Downing says, of the "marriage fantasy of security and wholeness" (1989, p. xxiv). Many of us are seeking a new paradigm or a way to transform an unhappy marriage to find something nourishing. This book is also offered to previous generations of women who felt trapped and could not leave or never had the opportunity to know deep love.

Many modern women have a default pattern of self-reliance, inclining toward remaining virginal, one-in-herself, toward never being vulnerable to a man the way our ancestral women were (though that was not what Harding intended with her definition). We took on the compensatory position of complete independence. And that might be fine, except that the true core value for many of us is that we love deep intimacy, closeness, relatedness, and sharing—and we love loving. We are beloveds of love. We want to trust; we want to have the courage and strength to be vulnerable and let love in rather than have to be defended and guarded. Many of us want those qualities, but few seem to possess them.

Moving toward the virginal (both puritanical and sovereign) often felt like a way of perpetuating my own compensatory pattern of not needing a man, of being invulnerable. In contrast, a wild woman is a fierce lover—a defender of a woman's instinct to partner and to love and to live with passion.

We also love our freedom, and partnering rapidly feels like an encroachment on that; but then we have to ask, "What is freedom?" It is freedom from those old ghosts of the past who dominate our psyches and prevent our full blossoming, including the blossoming through union with the inner masculine and with a man. It is freedom from being controlled by core wounds, complexes, and instinctual compulsions; those are the ultimate freedoms. Being in a relationship that is free of old ghosts would not feel restrictive, would not prevent us from being able to continue on our journeys of becoming. In fact, such a relationship would *support* the journey.

There are other kinds of freedom: freedom from responsibility and freedom to do what we want and when and with whom. Those have appeal, especially after we become mothers caring for young dependents. But those are not the ones I am tracking. We are strong women who choose our responsibilities based on the people and things we love; and even though such responsibilities are demanding, they also nourish us—our children, homes, pets, education, and work. Likewise, we choose with whom we want to share time and how we wish to spend that time because we value those people and activities. Freedom from the ghosts—the archetypes that are preventing us from our full blossoming—this is the deeper freedom, even though at times it may show up in other ways.

Most of my adult life, I carried shame and guilt for my sexuality. I also felt conflicted because sometimes I like wearing high heels and short skirts, and I enjoy sexual energy and feeling like a sexy woman for me, not for anyone else. It rarely felt OK to be sexy out loud; it triggered my self-judgment, and too often someone was nearby to mirror that self-reproach.

My patrilineal message about my sexuality was deeply wounding. I was an only child, and my father—in depth psychology language—projected his anima, or soul image, onto me, the idealized little daddy's girl. The message that imprinted was that in order to receive love, a woman must be the idealized projection of a man's soul, which teaches us to put ourselves in an inferior position of serving the man. Harding (1970) in *The Way of All Women* talks about anima women who either naively or unconsciously carry the soul image of a man. She refers to the phenomenon as something that happens to a woman by nature because of her father's projection. When a girl grows up being seen not as who she is but as her father's idealized image, that is her normal; she cannot know anything different. It is painful and complicated to repair and, in my case, it is related directly to my core wounding and fear of the vulnerability of loving a man.

A woman reared under the influence of a father's idealized projections risks losing the man she loves. By showing her true colors and by giving her reaction as close to present time as possible, the man she loves soon begins to discriminate between the woman and his anima, whether consciously or not. Many of us struggle to find our voices; we must learn to speak up and be seen for who we actually are. Further, we must learn how to speak up in ways that ensure we can be heard—and not with such intense reactivity that the other person is triggered and tries to silence us. When emotions are high, as with anger for example, neither person can effectively communicate with or hear the other. This is the work in day-to-day practice. And it is simply practice.

Women who carry father wounds can benefit from a reconciliation with their fathers if possible. When reconciliation is possible a positive intrapsychic father image can develop. Once healed, this inner figure can offer strength and guidance and a positive parental masculinity in both the inner and outer worlds. For some women, achieving rapprochement with the father can be problematic. Depending on the nature and severity of the wounding, the woman may have to come to terms with her father-relationship on her own. She may also benefit from a relationship with a therapist or positive male father-figure that offers a corrective experience. If the father was remorseful for his transgressions, forgiveness and acceptance become conceivable. In less injurious father-daughter relationships, it may be enough that the daughter develops her own voice, which then differentiates the woman from his anima projection.

Much of the healing of our sexuality and our voices is related to the healing of the inner father image that resulted from inadequate fathering; many women's poor self-image and inability to form lasting relationships stems from the father relationship. Paradoxically, that journey of healing the father wound culminates in finding the feminine spirit. Leonard (1982) arrives at the conclusion through the guidance of her dreams: "To redeem the father meant finding the feminine spirit in myself" (p. 167). As we heal the father wound, we simultaneously encounter the wild woman within. The inner masculine—whether as father, animus, or both—is intrinsic to the wounding and the healing, just as the wild woman archetype is as well. We must be open to the experience of the feminine and express it in our own unique ways. Previously, *men* defined femininity; now it is up to us women to define it for ourselves.

The Goddesses

I must acknowledge the Greek goddesses present in this book, my research and my own unfolding in whatever way they reveal themselves: Aphrodite, virgin goddess of sexuality, love, and beauty; Artemis, virgin goddess of bears, forests, and the wild; and Hera, goddess of marriage. Those three goddesses may be in conflict: one desiring sex, love, and beauty; one preferring forests and solitude; and one still holding on to the hope that both sex and deep intimacy are possible with one person—without losing a sense of self.

In addition, the Roman myth that weaves through my whole exploration is the story of Eros and Psyche, Love and Soul. In the tale, Psyche is a mortal whose beauty causes other mortals to make offerings to her rather than to Venus (Aphrodite). In her wrath, Venus creates a plot for her son Cupid (Eros) to have Psyche fall in love with a hideous monster. She is dressed in wedding and funeral attire for the event on the mountaintop. Cupid's arrow is intended for Psyche, to cause her to fall in love with a monster; however, he accidentally scratches himself with his own arrow causing him to promptly fall in love with Psyche. He does not reveal his identity to her and hides her away in his chamber where she is only with him in dark. After much cajoling, Eros permits Psyche a visit with her sisters; the sisters are seized with envy upon learning the true identity of Psyche's secret husband and tell her lies to cause her to believe her husband is a hideous monster. Psyche becomes curious until she is unable to respect her husband's wish that she never gaze upon his true form. At night, she gathers a knife to protect herself and then holds an oil lamp near him to reveal his identity as the god of Love. Having been betrayed, Cupid flees and leaves Psyche in a wake of shock and grief. She realizes her dreadful error and thus she begins her quest to find her beloved and win back his trust, with his child conceived and gestating inside her womb.

After much wandering, Psyche courageously goes to Cupid's mother, Venus, and begs her for mercy and guidance. Venus wickedly gives Psyche the first of four impossible tasks: to separate and sort a heap of various grains and seeds by dawn. Psyche collapses and cries in hopeless despair, but an ant takes pity on her and gathers an army of insects to help with the sorting. Venus is furious at the accomplishment and gives her a second impossible task: to collect wool from dangerous, aggressive mountain sheep. Realizing it is impossible and that she will die anyway, Psyche intends to throw herself in the river. Instead, a divinely inspired reed gives Psyche instructions to gather the wool from the briers rather than the sheep directly. In doing so, Psyche quietly manages to complete the second task. Venus, unsatisfied and harboring her grievous son in her castle, gives Psyche yet a third task: to collect water from the river Styx in a glass vessel. It is a foreboding cliff and once again, Psyche falls into despair. This time, Jupiter himself takes pity on her and sends his golden eagle to fight off the dragons and retrieve the water for her. Venus sends her on the fourth and final task that will surely finish her, a journey to the underworld to fetch a cask of Persephone's beauty ointment and bring it back to Venus. Again, realizing the task means certain death, Psyche climbs a tower intending to jump off and end her life. However, the tower speaks to her and gives her instructions on how to journey to the underworld: remain silent, do not aid others who are asking it of her; take honeyed cakes for the three-headed hound Cerberus (for coming and going); and take coins to pay the ferryman, for both directions. She does this, meets the Queen of the Underworld, does not linger too long, gets the ointment, and makes the return journey. (Almost.) She returns to the upper world and the light of day, only to be overcome by curiosity: she breaks Venus's rule—she opens the cask. This sends Psyche into a deep, unmoving sleep. Sensing her plight, Cupid is aroused to escape from his mother's tower and find his beloved. He wakes the sleeping Psyche with a kiss. She then delivers the cask to Venus completing her final task. Cupid appeals to the gods and the lovers are granted permission to be married on Olympus as immortal equals. Venus is appeased and Psyche gives birth to their daughter, Voluptas, whose name translates as "pleasure."

The tale is about learning the tasks, completing the arduous journey to Hades and back and then eventually, the *coniunctio* or sacred marriage of the pair. Even though this book is about the lived experience of relationship and loving, that is one level; the underlying personal work has a more internal nature and is about the psychological union of two. At the end of the myth, Psyche gives birth to Pleasure, their girl-child (well, that sounds inspiring). We cannot speak of that myth without speaking of Aphrodite and how Psyche must win Aphrodite's favor by accomplishing her tasks and gaining wisdom.

The myth of Eros and Psyche defines our current model of romantic love and demonstrates the dominant paradigm. The current traditional form of the long-term, heterosexual, monogamous relationship is not working for many couples. For example, much of my therapy practice focuses on relationship problems, and more than half of marriages end in divorce. The National Center for Health Statistics (1991) reported that from 1975 to 1988 in the United States, wives initiated divorces approximately two-thirds of the time; they were women who had been living in families with children and who faced great financial challenge after divorce. Women are rebelling—even at great risk and cost. Maybe we are too choosy or our expectations of our partners are too high, or likely it is the other way around: that the expectations of us—and that we place on ourselves—are too high and therefore not sustainable. During my divorce in Canada, my lawyer said that in her family law practice, women initiate the divorce 80% of the time.

A new paradigm can emerge for two people who are courageous and are doing their personal work of individuating—both separately and together. One definition of individuation that Jung offered is that it is the process of becoming a whole person who is indivisible—can no longer be divided—as paradoxical opposites become reconciled. What does it look like for two "I's" to be in a relationship as a "we"—for two individuals who are individuating and becoming self-conscious to navigate the paradox of separate and together?

My orientation to this work is through the field of depth psychology, founded by Carl Jung. It is a psychology that serves the soul or psyche. The Greek word for soul is *psyche*, and *study* or *knowledge of* is *-logia*. Depth psychology then is an exploration of what is going on in a person's psychological depths, or in the person's soul. This book seeks to bring out of the collective cultural shadow women's innate wildness and conscious relationship to their instincts, a birthright that gets socialized out of girls. In bringing this archetype out of shadow for women, women will instinctively be led to questions—and eventually their own answers—about alternative paradigms regarding attitudes about sexuality and relationships.

An important tenet of this book and depth psychology in general is the Jungian concept of individuation. It involves becoming our most authentic self, wherein the relationship of the ego to the Self changes. In other words, the old, egocentric way of life gets reorganized around the Self. As a woman is in the process of individuation—which entails, among other things, differentiation from culture—she is called to explore her authentic, wild and innate: sexuality, relationships, values, and paradigms. As she becomes conscious of the cultural matrix, the dominant paradigm may no longer fit or it may need to be reimagined.

The originating question that is guiding this exploration is: *What are some of the ways a woman who has recovered the wild woman archetype expresses her sexuality and engages in relationships?* Relationship is referring to a significant partner, person, or people in a woman's life. Some women will choose not to have one single partner, whereas others will choose to have one significant partner, and the individuals involved (not the cultural ideals) will define the parameters of that relationship. Some of us will continue to prefer the heterosexual model, whereas others will choose homosexual or bisexual love. Some prefer non-monogamous paradigms with one significant partner; while others will choose more than one significant partner; and still others will prefer no partner at all. There are many possible variations. Also, we may think we have our preference, but something else may come along and then we must adapt to what life provides. Such frustration can serve as a catalyst for examining our complexes and our individuation process. That was my experience, and in truth that frustration was both the catalyst and the source of the energy from which this book emerged.

Regarding homosexuality and the matter of whether it is an innate part of one's sexuality or a choice, this book is not attempting to answer that question. My concern is that women should be free to express and experience their sexuality in ways that feel authentic for them. My tendency—and therefore this book—is primarily toward heterosexuality, but I view sexuality as a spectrum and seldom to be wholly one way or the other. There is space for openness and fluidity whereby a woman can explore what works for her and that may change as her life changes. I will henceforth use the singular word *relationship* to recognize all of the aforementioned possibilities, including *relationships* as plural, or no relationship at all.

Alchemy

Alchemy is a complex and mysterious body of knowledge that involves symbolically turning base metal into gold; it is a process of transformation. Simply stated, alchemy is aligned with the Jungian concept of individuation as, in part, it involves becoming conscious of the instinctual sphere. As we lean into the muck of our lives—the hard stuff, the base metal—we engage in a psychological transformation process that actualizes what is valuable, the gold. As the research methodology for this book involves alchemical hermeneutics, and as the topic is on the instinctual wild woman, it is valuable to consider alchemy and instincts in more detail.

For modern women, the problem is, ultimately, that we have become too far removed from the wild woman archetype; we have become too removed from our own good feminine instinctual nature. I use the word *good* here, but archetypes are ambivalent; and that will be explored further. We require a moral code or spiritual ground to counterbalance the purely instinct state; however, in a society that can be too puritanical, we can over-compensate and the ego can become too disconnected from the natural ground of the instincts. Domestication has caused many women to become too removed from the wild woman who contains the natural instincts. The wild woman archetype can be expressed through a woman's behavior; the wild woman can be actualized both in the psyche and in a woman's lived experience.

Part of the individuation process includes the union or reconciliation of opposites; the spiritual life and the instinctual life can become such a pair of opposites that require unification. Although the process of individuation is unique for each person, in alchemy certain symbolic procedures and stages guide the process, and we will look at them briefly. In *Mysterium Coniunctionis*, Jung (1955-56/1976) wrote about the stages of the mystical union of opposites as the central idea of the alchemical procedure as outlined by alchemist Gerhard Dorn. There is a preliminary stage during which we are basically whole but in a state of unconsciousness; that stage is the *unio naturalis*. In that state, we function from the instinctual sphere; it is a preconscious condition of wholeness. Jung refers to it as a dark unity, not illuminated by conscious awareness. It is a stage of *participation mystique*, a term Lucien Lévy-Bruhl used to describe a condition in which the individual is indistinct from the environment and entirely unaware of instincts. The personality remains unconsciously identified with the archetypes, or unconscious forces, that drive motivations. In this stage, there is no differentiation between the individual identity and other. While some differentiation evolves through the first half of life, the person remains largely affected by the archetypes in the unconscious and is unable to differentiate the archetypal affects from the conscious ego personality. This stage continues until the individuation process fully begins after the ego is, hopefully, strong enough—typically in midlife. It can be represented in the well-known phrase *ignorance is bliss*.

Following that preliminary stage in alchemy are three principal stages of development, according to Dorn, that lead to the eventual *mysterium coniunctionis* (sacred union). The first stage is that of the *unio mentalis* (mental union). Dorn wrote, "meditative philosophy consists in the overcoming of the body by mental union (*unio mentalis*)" (Jung, 1955-56/1976, p. 465). This stage is about self-reflection and becoming aware of the instinctual drives; ultimately, the goal of this stage is to free the soul from matter. Or, to put it in more practical terms, to learn to differentiate and attune to the still, quiet voice of the soul from the powerful voices of the instincts, with their appetites and drives. This stage is paradoxical in that it is the first step toward reunion even though it involves further separation and differentiation. We want to differentiate the instincts as they come upon us, neither repressing them nor being overtaken by them. We want to be able to experience the power of the instincts—but with consciousness. We aim for transcending the body's affectivity and instinctuality.

When confronted with an instinctual drive, we must stand strong and respectfully, remembering we are in the presence of a force greater than the individual ego. Keiron Le Grice elaborated:

> The *unio mentalis* marks a separation from a condition of identity with the archetypes/instincts. We might have previously been acting out Bear archetype and then, to effect the *unio mentalis*, consciousness would need to step outside of the instinctual Bear pattern and engage with it. In this way, the inherent "spiritual" aspect of that instinct could be liberated/separated from the instinctual. The union of ego-consciousness with the liberated "spiritual" aspect of the instinct is the *unio mentalis*. (K. Le Grice, personal communication, 2013)

If we imagine an instinctual drive as the image of Bear, we do not want it to attack and overtake us, so we must gauge its reaction to us, observe it from a respectful distance, and maybe even track it so we can learn about its behaviors. In this stage, we want to *observe*.

The second stage is achieved when the soul rejoins the body; here the *unio mentalis* and the body unite with consciousness intact rather than via a regression to the previous, unconscious condition. This involves the withdrawal of projections through laborious and patient work with the unconscious through dreams and active imagination. Jung (1976) wrote of this stage, "Dorn 'shaped out' his intuition of a mysterious center pre-existent man, which at the same time represented a cosmos, i.e., a totality, while he himself remained conscious that he was portraying the *self* in matter" (p. 532). Jung connects this to the Self symbols—in particular, those revealed in mandalas.

This is the point where the individual psychological structure has become reorganized around the Self as in Edinger's (1991) image where the ego-Self axis has become established and the ego is in service to the greater whole of the Self. The individual now finds the sense of security and wholeness from connection to that source and being attuned to it. Soul is freed from the instincts, with consciousness intact, during the *unio mentalis*, and we come to the awareness that our very beings are portraying the self in matter. It sounds like it is a quick, neat process, but it is not; we seem to endure one test after another to return to our mysterious center. Because of that repetition, it can feel as if the *nigredo* (blackening or death) experience is one challenge after another, somewhat relentlessly, and that it can go on for years.

The third stage, the *mysterium coniunctionis*, is about returning to the state of wholeness or oneness with the cosmos or the unitary ground of existence. This stage transcends that of Jung's individuation opus; it is the domain of the alchemists. "A consummation of the *mysterium coniunctionis* can be expected only when the unity of the spirit, soul, and body is made one with the original *unus mundus*" (Jung, 1976, p. 465). This makes for the ultimate union and harmony between the individual and the cosmos. It can be attained for fleeting, transcendent moments, but it is doubtful that it is ever fully realized, perhaps with rare exceptions. As speculation, it seems plausible that with achievement of the totality of the second stage, that third stage may happen naturally.

Classical alchemy describes the *magnum opus* of transformation in four color stages: *nigredo* (blackening); *albedo* (whitening); *citrinitas* (yellowing); and *rubedo* (reddening). The *nigredo* is the darkening and longest phase, and can be represented by depression and symbolic death. It is in this stage that the *prima materia* or base metal decays and decomposes. Here we confront the shadow aspects of the personality, all the parts of ourselves that we reject and push away. It is a state of undifferentiated awareness and the state of the *unio naturalis*. It is a dark time in life and one is unaware of the unconscious. One must traverse the dark night of the soul terrain until eventually, psychologically, the *albedo* emerges. This stage of whitening is a brief stage of purification during which the individual becomes aware of contrasexual images in the psyche such as the anima and animus, and insights into shadow material are realized. The *citrinitas* phase is not so commonly considered in modern time, but historically it has heralded the solar dawning and the awareness of the archetypal presences of the wise old man and wise old woman. The *rubedo* is the final stage of the alchemical procedure and heralds the Self, or awareness of the totality of the psyche. It is the stage where new life, new red blood, enlivens the person and it is the completion of the rebirth in the transformation process—this signals the gold or Philosopher's Stone at the end of the great work. It is the *mysterium coniunctionis*.

A complex part of alchemy covers sulfur and the instincts; in fact, it is through our conscious holding of the instincts that we move toward individuation. Transforming the instinct is connected alchemically to sulfur. Sulfur can be imagined as the flammable, compulsive element of instincts and desires when they arise. It refers to being in the grip of a drive or desire and being possessed by it: we can get so excited by the object of our desire that we lose ourselves in the desire. Think of the experience of falling in love; the intoxicating element that adds to the rush of desire is considered sulfur in alchemy. Any form of addiction or compulsive behavior is also a signal that sulfur is present. The ego engages with these desires and impulses and transforms the compulsion, sometimes into emotion. Through this process, the Self emerges. Without consciousness to contain and differentiate the compulsion, the ego will simply fall into unconsciousness again, all the work of the *unio mentalis* will be lost, and the process will have to start over. Consciousness is essential in order to stand outside of the instinct. It requires a moral code or personal commitment so that a woman can exercise her power of choice and not be swept along by the pull of the instinct. Her moral code standing against the instinct creates a tension of the opposites that enables the conscious woman to make an empowered conscious choice.

The compulsion-sulfur must be burned off from the desire so that the ideal condition is one of experiencing the instinctual desire but not surrendering to it: we want to remain separate and objective so that we can activate the power of choice. We can learn to separate out the compulsive element from the full rush of desire so the passion is not lost. Ideally, this is done with equanimity so as not to be thrown off balance. We do not want to lose the instinctual desire; we want to expunge the compulsive element so that a woman can consciously give herself over to the desire—just let it be expressed without control, safe in the knowledge that the destructive, extreme, possessive nature of the desire has been overcome. The more one can overcome compulsion the more one is able to let go of rational egoic control.

Anyone who has been conscious while in the grip of a compulsion knows it is not easily overcome at all. Further, we may have conflicting, competing compulsions at one time. For instance, we may become aware of our compulsive, instinctual desire for a relationship as well as our defenses that prevent anyone from getting close; and we then find that both of those sulfuric instincts are in conflict. Both are also qualities of the feminine: relatedness and fierce protection. Experience teaches us the agony of heartbreak and betrayal. Love can become terrifying because we know the whole experience: the bliss of giving ourselves over to the compulsive desire, but we also know the potential pain of it too. We can become so afraid of heartbreak or of losing ourselves again that we avoid intimacy. When that happens, we move toward that I-don't-need-a-man instinct to defend our hearts. If given the opportunity to choose, we want to be conscious of both instincts operating and exercise our power of choice from there.

Some instincts that are helpful, like those belonging to the wild woman archetype, have to be recovered out of shadow, whereas other instincts carry so much compulsion that they have to be handled with care and explored for their symbolic or metaphoric meaning. For example, *spirits* for a hard alcohol addiction can be the human spirit seeking a connection to a spiritual life, or it could be the human spirit in search of itself. Other examples, are food for a difficult mother relationship because the mother is the original source of sustenance and nurturance. Cocaine for a disempowerment wound because it provides a sense of feeling powerful and focused. Opioids for an emotional or physical wound because they relieve pain. Exploring the compulsive substance for its deeper meaning allows for greater understanding of the wound and helps bring it out of shadow for increased possibility of healing. Instincts must be differentiated and related to as separate from the individual personality; otherwise individuals risk becoming possessed by these archetypal energies. Our work is to face those instincts squarely and not regress back to an unconscious state.

Joseph Campbell spoke of learning to ride the back of the Dionysian leopard. Dionysus is the Greek god of wine, ecstasy, and madness; in modern days, we can experience him as the lascivious energy found at music festivals such as Burning Man, but otherwise, he is largely repressed—probably due to Christian morality—or out of the shadow he comes through in unconscious obsessions and compulsive behavior (women's addiction to wine). In harmony with that recognition, I had a dream.

> *I am with several others in a corridor that is like an alchemical laboratory. A secret door opened and a tiger is released into the corridor. I spot it crouched down, ready to pounce. It is after me! I'm scared and call for help, but no one comes. We somehow rollick and frolic and barrel down the long corridor. The animal could easily shred me, but it doesn't. We roll and tumble. I know I have to just keep going with it until it is played out.*

I awake and am surprised the tiger has not mauled me. What it wanted was for me to play with it. To *play*. I immediately picture cats in the wild. They roll around in a fur pile all the time and are very playful. Even though I was scared in the dream, I awoke feeling vibrant and playful, recognizing that I have been too serious under the weight of too many responsibilities. Many of us even feel guilty for making time to play. We need to frolic amidst the seriousness of grounded life. If we do not play, our playful tiger instinct will become destructive and harmful. In my dream, there was no way I could get on the back of that tiger and ride it out, nor could I get away from it, nor was anyone going to intervene—but I was able to engage with it in a way that satisfied it.

The process of alchemical transformation is a map we can refer to that helps us understand the individuation process. In an oversimplified summary, we ultimately want to get to the state where we can stand consciously with our ideals and values on one side and our instinctual drives on the other. We want to strive to hold these two opposites in balance and not be too far one way or the other.

Bear

Before and during the writing of this book, which was also a catalyst for my personal work, I had numerous experiences with bears, both in dreams and in life, and as my work progressed, the experiences became more integrated into consciousness. I was working with Bear in earnest for a few years, having initially understood Bear to be a symbolic representation of the bear-man with whom I was enamored in life. He was an animus man initially—the idealized image of my inner masculine—and then ensued years of struggle to differentiate the man from my animus, until finally the grip released and we became simple friends. I initially understood him as Bear in my dreams because he was the first man I fell in love with after divorce and, at that time, I was more afraid of the vulnerability of love than I was afraid of bears. In addition, he was a wild, mountain man himself, spending much of his time wandering off into the woods for days.

I was studying ecopsychology and reading Terry Tempest Williams's (1994) "Undressing the Bear," when I had an aha moment. In Williams's work, Bear became so much more than I had initially perceived; Bear was also the wild feminine, the wild woman. I was Bear as much as my animus man was. I had this dream.

I am tending my horse at my farmhouse on acreage that blends into wild land. A mama duck leads her babies near the hooves of the big horse. The horse backs up from the ducks to give them room as they learn their new environment. I worry for them—so vulnerable near those huge hooves—but I am somehow informed that this is how it works: we all learn how to move together in the world, and we all teach each other. I look out to the field and see the mama bear and her cub. She is always there; she lives on the land, we know each other well, and we maintain a respectful distance. It's a solace to see her there. But then she is coming for me. I go to hide in the house, but the door is a swinging type that doesn't close— the inside and outside are easily enterable. I try to squeeze into a little square cupboard, but a big square box is filling the space. I know she is going to find me. She comes into the house; we look at each other, and she turns into a woman. I recognize the woman. She is me!

This dream did not have the feel of being overtaken by instincts, nor was that happening in my life. It did have the feel of reclaiming my previously repressed feminine instinctual nature and integrating it fully into my conscious body. At that time in my life, I was deciding to write about the wild woman as an archetype that is a fierce protector of a woman's instincts for relationship for intimacy, and for mothering. It was as if the wild woman archetype was agreeing to work *with* me, *through* me, for my writing and research work. I observe her; therefore, I am still differentiated from her, but I am also becoming her. This describes the nature of the creative process of writing about her: the words come, but "I" do not bid them to come. This may sound like a possession; possibly it *is* a positive example of possession or of being overtaken by an instinct, but it felt affirming. It was also undertaken consciously. By being conscious and observing the instinctual energies, I am possessed while remaining separate from them. That leads us closer to a greater union with the *mysterium*: just by being in such close relationship, consciously, with a figure from the archetypal and in-stinctual realm.

CHAPTER 2
The Wild Woman Archetype

To embrace the Feminine is to embrace paradox. Paradox preserves mystery, and mystery inspires belief. . . . I see the Feminine defined as a reconnection to the Self, a commitment to the wildness within—our instincts, our capacity to create and destroy; our hunger for connection as well as sovereignty, interdependence and independence, at once. . . . I believe in the power of Bear.

Terry Tempest Williams, 1994, p. 53

This chapter invokes the wild woman archetype intentionally and consciously and invites her voice into this book. Asking the wild woman to fit into a structured document is perhaps an oxymoron; nevertheless, if we are patient, fluid, and quiet, she will come. In addition to invoking her, we will create a definition of her—or allow her to do that for us. Next, we descend more deeply into the definition of wild by reviewing ecopsychology literature and exploring the relationship between women and nature. We consider a new cosmology that includes a valuing of the feminine individually and collectively. We also look at Greek goddess Artemis as the protectress of the inviolable, absolute feminine. In addition, throughout, we explore experiences, dreams, and synchronicities, as well as relevant active imaginations, with the wild woman—as part of the practice of transference dialogues congruent with the alchemical hermeneutics approach. Transference dialogues constitute a way of engaging directly with the material of the psyche to let the unconscious have a voice and to honor the soul in the book.

To introduce and invoke the wild woman archetype, I want to share an actual encounter.

I was in the Peruvian Amazon, walking down a long, straight, red clay road after a flash rainfall that had turned the road into a slippery track of deep mud. The mud sucked the sandals off my feet, so I plucked along barefoot. The noonday sun burned off the rain clouds and made the wet ground emit mirage vapor. I caught a glimpse of a wisp of a person, whom I picked my way toward for 20 minutes before reaching her. She was ancient. And she was frail, at about a hundred pounds, but full of heat and life. Her black hair was long and crazy, and her smile was missing lots of teeth. In the most natural way, we faced each other and laughed at our muddy feet. She was Shipibo and could not speak English— only a little Spanish. I speak English and only a smattering of Spanish. We rested under a shade tree, giggling and nattering as though we understood the other perfectly, and actually we did, just not the words. I offered her water; she reciprocated with something like an oatcake that we shared. Then she rummaged in her cloth bag and pulled out her handicrafts: beaded bracelets and colorfully embroidered cloth. The patterns, I knew, had come from plant medicine visions. She wanted me to have a beaded cuff with a butterfly pattern: "Medicina para el corazón" (Medicine for the heart). She patted her heart and nodded, indicating my heart. I gave her Peruvian soles in exchange. Near the end of our encounter, she told me her name: "María. Mama de Guillermo." I knew this woman by reputation because I had studied Peruvian folk medicine under her son, Guillermo, who had learned it from her. She was the maestro's mother and teacher and an extraordinary curandera, or medicine woman. Her solo journey to visit her son would take many days by boat and by foot from her home in the remote jungle.

This spry little female creature, nearly one hundred years old, occurred to me as "pure animal woman" and as much a part of the jungle and wild nature as any human I could imagine.

Our encounter happened about four years before this research, but, as can happen with real-life experiences, Maria moved into my inner psychic life and became "the wild woman," available for me to visit in my imagination as one face of the wild woman.

Initial View

The Initial View sections of each chapter take a preliminary, sweeping glance across the existing literature that informs this book. The popularity of Estés' book when it came out—and still today, almost 25 years later—should demonstrate how needed that archetype is in our Western culture. It is a rare accomplishment for any depth psychology author to be so widely received in the mainstream. The recovery of the wild woman archetype clearly strikes a chord with many women. She is available to us at birth but civilizing and rigid roles have caused us to neglect our relationship with her to the extent that we no longer understand how to relate to her wildness. Propriety and over-domestication outcast her to the forest edge where she is lurking, her black fur glinting now and again, as she watches for her chance to approach. We experience her instinctual nature in certain psychic characteristics that are mimicked by other wild creatures: keen sensing, playful spirit, heightened capacity for devotion, relational by nature, inquiring, possessed of great endurance and strength, deeply intuitive, intensely concerned with their young, their mate, and their pack.

We need to understand this wildness more. To deepen the definition of *wild*, we turn to readings from ecopsychology, which relates to nature as a mirror for our individual psyches in connection with the wild feminine. In "Undressing the Bear," Williams (1994) connects the powerful instinctual animal body of the bear to the wild feminine.

> To embrace the Feminine is to embrace paradox. Paradox preserves mystery, and mystery inspires belief. . . . I see the Feminine defined as a reconnection to the Self, a commitment to the wildness within—our instincts, our capacity to create and destroy; our hunger for connection as well as sovereignty, interdependence and independence, at once. . . . I believe in the power of Bear. (p. 53)

That quote speaks to all of the complexity—and captures the essence—of this book. It takes the strength of a wild bear woman to hold the tension of these paradoxes. The wild feminine needs to be embraced and continuously related to—for many if not all of us. The wound to the wildness in women and society seems so pervasive culturally that coming into relationship with the paradox of Bear seems essential to healing individually and collectively. With a society dominated by an overly conservative patriarchy, we now more than ever need to come into relationship with our healthy instinctual feminine wildness as a corrective.

The term, *wild woman*, describes an a *priori* force available to all women whose development is restricted within the frame of the patriarchal culture. Also, this archetype, like many archetypes, may constellate only as a woman matures and is no longer content living within the dominant paradigm because she is further along in the individuation process. Archetypes are the ever-present and biologically necessary regulators of the instinctual sphere whose range of action covers the whole realm of the psyche and loses its absoluteness only when limited by the relative freedom of the will. As we become more conscious—and further along in the individuation process—we can become aware of the archetypes and their instinctual drives that are present and acting upon us. It is with our consciousness that we can exercise our will to disrupt archetypal patterns that are unconscious and autonomous. The ideal is to be engaged with the instinctual realm but consciously—to be engaged with the wild woman archetype consciously. We do not benefit from having her pounce on us in our unawares, for example. We want to develop a relationship to her because she contains the *good* and needed instincts of the feminine.

At this point, let us go back to the matter of archetypal ambivalence since I am asserting that the wild woman contains *good* instincts. The appropriate questions with regard to that assertion are these: "Are the wild woman's instincts always *good*?" and "What does the nongenerative form or the shadow expression of the wild woman look like?" Archetypes, as *a priori* forces, are neither wholly good nor wholly bad; they are inherently ambivalent. We can imagine them as energy fields that just are. They are closely related to the instinctual sphere. In that way, the instincts of the wild woman cannot always be considered to be generative and good. We must exercise our will to invoke her, become conscious of her, and relate to her—just as we might a bear. For example, if we stumble upon a bear in the forest and separate her from her cubs, we will likely have a negative experience. On the other hand, if we get to know the bear's patterns and behaviors, we may enjoy a relationship to this powerful force of nature. How does that show up psychologically? The wild woman gets socialized out of women and repressed into the shadow, and if women are not allowed to express their wildness, it can show up in the forms of compulsions or obsessions—the alchemical sulfur. The obsessive component overlaps with the psychological act of projection, whereby a woman might become obsessed with a man who bears her animus projection; and then all her thoughts and psychic energy get directed to that man. The compulsive behaviors may grab hold of a woman and erupt out of her: perhaps as a shopping spree, a bottle of wine, a joint, an eating binge, a lurid sexual encounter, or an affair—something that breaks the safety and harmony of her narrow and well-manicured life. That is what it can look like when she unexpectedly pounces to try and get our attention.

Such eruptions are similar to the emergence of Dionysus, who resides largely in the shadow. These eruptions are related to the Christianized Western culture. Dionysus is a half-mortal, half-god figure who is known as the deity of ecstasy, wine, madness, and women.

Dionysus comes in at this point in the discussion of the wild woman because I have an intuitive sense that the two know each other well. For example, recall the dream of the tiger that wanted to "rollick and frolic" down the alchemical corridor to encourage more play. Ecstasy and play can be closely related, and both are often forgotten. These joyful expressions connect us to the long-forgotten part of ourselves that makes us feel alive, vital, and connected with every living thing. Over–civilization causes a woman to be unable to freely express her wildness and give herself over to ecstatic bliss with the Dionysian spirit—particularly if she is still largely unconscious or has children to be responsible for. Or if her Dionysian spirit erupts, it is usually in a shadow or a compulsive form of behavior that can be shameful and destructive. Younger women and girls are still close to that spiritedness; however, without consciousness, they are acting only from archetypal possession and not from a sense of differentiation from the archetype or instinct; they are in the stage of *participation mystique*.

We are discussing the wild woman as the archetype that is representative of a woman's instinctive nature, but she is more than that. She is the natural psyche and the innate, basic nature of women. She is indigenous. She is our intrinsic nature. The image of meeting María, the "indigenous" healer woman, the pure animal woman, is mytholo-gized in my psyche as a personification of this archetype, though there are other personifications as well. The wild woman is more than a single archetype in the psyche; she is the essential feminine. In relationship to her, we gain access to our own instinctive nature as animal women. I met María shortly after leaving the role of wife out of a feeling of having become over-domesticated. I was discovering a relationship to that wildish womanliness that would no longer be contained in the patriarchal cage. Meeting María felt surreal, like a veil had parted, to reencounter the wild feminine nature within me. I had lived with that archetype before, when I was a carefree young woman exploring the world and riding a motorbike; but I was not conscious and I certainly never had a relationship to her—that was the stage of *participation mystique*.

After marriage, many of us describe feeling that we lose ourselves, but what many of us have lost is a connection to the wild woman. We lose her because we never had consciousness of her; perhaps we were possessed by her, but we were not in relationship to her. She feels so intrinsic to our deep nature that we experience disconnection from her as a loss of self. In the bleakest days of over-domestication, it can feel as though the soul has flown off and there is an urgency to find her. Once rediscovered, we can be sure not to lose connection with her twice. We come to know that with her our lives blossom, our relationships grow in depth, our mothering thrives, our work is inspired and meaningful, we find joy and playfulness, we are the guardians of hearth and home, and we know respect from self and others. We fight hard to keep the wild woman once we recover her. Passion to keep contact with this wild aspect is perhaps what, ironically, has kept me unpartnered for an extended period. Ironic, because one of the qualities of the wild woman is the desire to partner and be concerned with her mate, and yet there is also a real fear of losing a sense of self and becoming over-domesticated *again*. As well, there are many creative ways to blossom in life, relationship is only one of them. In my experience, re-establishing a relationship to this archetype has not improved my romantic relationships or sexual experiences. The wild woman's keen sense of knowing, intuition, and instincts do not necessarily make relationships clear so that we now know "what to do." The process still unfolds, the chaos still swirls, the challenges still arise, and the conflicting inner voices saying, "Stick it out" or "Run away" still echo in our now pointed ears. There is a multiplicity of voices rather than *one* inner voice, and we are required to consciously choose which to abide by. She has many faces.

James Hillman (1989) is another renowned depth psychotherapist who offered us archetypal psychology and with it, a polytheistic perspective. Polytheism acknowledges that there are many truths and many inner voices and that, despite our desire for clarity, not all of them agree. In Hillman's view, the psyche or soul has many directions and sources of meaning, which can feel like an ongoing state of conflict—a struggle with one's *daimones*. A polytheistic perspective acknowledges that ongoing inner conflict is a normal condition of the human psyche which leads to greater awareness and in time gives sacred differentiation to the turmoil. The task, the *work*, of individuation and alchemical transformation lies in differentiating the voices and listening to each and enduring being in the *massa confusa*, or clutter, for a time. Differentiating the plurality of voices in one's psyche can be painstaking and requires patience. Uncertainty, chaos, and confusion are all qualities of the moon-time feminine rather than the solar masculine. Paradoxically, the more we relate with the feminine, the more we can know the next step and the more we can know what to do in the moment—without trying so hard to have it *all* figured out—and the more we can become able to make a clear decision. The wild woman's way of knowing is a moment-by-moment way of knowing or choosing.

In contrast to polytheism, the Self, according to Jung, is the singular archetype of wholeness and totality where all opposites are reconciled. As a mandala image, it is both the center and the circumference; it is the telos of the individuation process, ultimately uniting consciousness with the unconscious. The Self is the totality and organizing center of the whole psyche, as opposed to the ego, which constitutes only a small part—the conscious part—and is like the proverbial tip of the iceberg. Jung's way of understanding the ego differed from Eastern approaches that encourage the transcendence of ego desires. That suggestion is more akin to burning off the sulfuric element from an instinctual desire for differentiation during the work of individuation. From a classical Jungian perspective, the totality of the realized Self then would contain the wild woman archetype, as well as a masculine counterpart, or whichever other archetypal opposite surfaced in the psyche, along with all other archetypal opposites.

However, from the perspective of archetypal psychology, the Self as a symbol of totality, unity, and wholeness gets deconstructed in favor of personifying or imagining—in favor of psyche or the wild woman. Hillman (1989) invites us to bring the imaginal perspective, the fantasy, to all that we see. Which means nothing less than dethroning the dominant fantasy ruling our view of the world as ultimately a unity—that real meaning, real beauty and truth require a unified vision. It also means that we would abandon a notion of our personality as ultimately a unity of self. Hillman suggests that instead of trying to cure pathological fragmentation wherever it appears, we would let the content of this fantasy cure consciousness of its obsession with unity. That also means we reframe the fantasy of what it means to be healthy and healed. I comfortably move in and out of the dominant fantasy of unity versus a perspective of multiplicity and polytheism. We can entertain both a Self-image of striving for wholeness as well as a pluralistic vision of a world ensouled and related to with the imagination. Hillman suggests that along with the departing dominant unitary fantasy would go its dominant emotion—loneliness—because we come to realize we are never alone in an ensouled world.

This book uses the symbolic fantasy of an essentially feminine principle and an essentially masculine principle as a way of personifying qualities of the psyche, though that fantasy is only one such way to imagine the concept. Ultimately, all the fantasies about how to imagine this belong to the wild woman of the psyche because she is the fantasy maker; there really is no right or wrong. It is a matter of whatever fantasy seems to resonate and of moving toward liberation from the dominant fantasy and patriarchal paradigm on many levels, including the totality, wholeness, and unity fantasy. We want to be fluid about that fantasy. Although this book is dominantly in the fantasy of engendered polarity, there is a caveat: *that even the masculine personifications, such as puer, animus, or even Eros, are ultimately all fantasy images that belong to the wild woman, the image-creating soul.* Though archetypes themselves are entirely real and autonomous forces, the image that personifies them is offered from the psyche. The idea that the anima (or the wild woman) is the one who creates the fantasy images was conceived by Hillman (1976). The wild woman is the personification of the soul that animates the imagination and is the spinner of fantasy of all unknown psychic capacities that lie waiting, drawing us seductively, uncannily inward to the dark of the uncut forest. Her task is to draw us closer to her reality, for to explore anima country is to venture toward the unknown, away from the comforts of what the ego is conscious of, and away from the safety of the familiar—even away from clear and crisp definitions.

Freud too emphasized the unconscious instinctual drives within the individual personality. He called it the id and likened it to chaos or a cauldron full of seething excitations. He described it as filled with energy from the instincts, but without organization, and only a striving to bring about the satisfaction of the instinctual needs subject to the observance of the pleasure principle. Freud, as most people know, was fond of the pleasure principle. The id is not entirely interchangeable with the wild woman archetype, but because of the closeness with the instinctual, animal realm, id energy is an important part of her. The fundamental difference is Freud's focus on the pleasure principle of seeking immediate pleasure and gratification and striving to avoid pain. The wild woman archetype is more eclectic than only that. Ultimately, she pursues what she loves: love and relationship. Though it is interesting that through much pain, Psyche and Eros do eventually give birth to Pleasure—it is possible the id and the wild woman are closer than we like to think, but not quite the way Freud meant, either.

We continue to reach for her definition as she is so expansive. She is all that is of instinct, she is worlds both seen and hidden, she is the image-maker and fantasy spinner, she is the animator of our being and lives. She is the female soul. She is something akin to the anima. The wild woman incorporates the female soul, the feminine soul, the psyche, and the anima; they are all aspects of the same. Anima is not limited to being part of male psychology; she is the personification of the human soul, of the psyche, and is present in both men and women. Anima is personified as feminine in both men and women, and it appears that is so regardless of gender or sexual orientation. The anima is an aspect of the wild woman. The anima is the psyche personified, as Psyche in the ancient story by Apuleius. The wild woman, too, is psyche personified and she is fittingly, paradoxically, one and many.

She fits within the multifaceted perspective of archetypal psychology because of her many faces.

> Anima means both psyche and soul, and we meet her in her numerous embodiments as soul of waters without whom we are dry, as soul of vegetation who greens our hope or blight with symptoms, as Lady of the Beasts riding our passions. . . . She is also a worrying succubus drawing off our life's juice, a harpy with talons, a cold white wraith with mad addictions. . . . And she is also the Sophia of wisdom, the Maria of compassion, the Persephone of destruction, compelling Necessity and Fate, and the Muse. (Hillman, 1976, pp. 42-43)

The wild woman, as the personification of the female soul, is all of that and more.

There is a risk worth addressing (but perhaps it is still reflecting my movement in and out of the mono-totality fantasy of the Self): that a psychology, a perspective, and a new paradigm that are in service to the soul run the risk of becoming just another monotheistic fantasy. Instead of being in service to the Self, the fantasy becomes a matter of being in service to the soul. To pose that as a question: Does the anima/soul/psyche run the risk of becoming another monotheistic fantasy replacing the Self fantasy? There is a difference, though, and that is the soul's connection with embodiment and imagination—and maybe that difference is everything. We necessarily need to hold—and move in and out of—those two fantasies: one representing spirit, ascension, and disembodiment (and which is dominant) and the other representing soul, descent, and embodiment (and which is emergent).

María came toward me as if a mirage. She could easily have turned to smoke and slipped away at that early stage of retrieving her in my intrapsychic life. The wild woman engenders every important facet of womanliness; she goes by many names, not only in order to peer into the myriad aspects of her nature but also to hold on to her. In the beginning of retrieving our relationship with the wild woman, she can turn to smoke in an instant; by naming her, we create for her a territory, says Estés. What if when I met María I had not stopped on the road, not laughed at our muddy feet, not offered her water, and not engaged in reciprocal exchange? *What if she had not told me her name?*—which was the last gift she offered at the end of our encounter. I would not have recognized her as the wise old medicine woman, the pure animal woman, pure *anima*-lity woman who animates life; she could have turned to smoke and vanished back into unconsciousness once more. Instead, she moved into my psyche as one of the myriad faces of the wild woman, the essential feminine—the human soul.

Lions and Tigers and Bears, and a Surfing Yogini

Brown bears have an interesting quality: they use the same trail over and over for *generations*. In fact, they place their feet in same tracks as the bears that went before them, leaving a pattern of depressions that are deep and ancient—particularly around the marking of trees to delineate their territories. One can imagine how it upsets their ecosystem and instincts when humans develop land and encroach on their pathways; no wonder they become disoriented. Psychically and in the collective, the wild woman is a little discombobulated and is padding out a new path.

An initial word about *wild*. This is not wild in the good-girls-gone-bad sense or its modern pejorative sense, meaning out of control, but in its original sense, which means to live a natural life, one with good instincts, respect, and healthy boundaries. *Wild* means a way of being natural but also conscious of our instinctual nature as animal women. *Wild* can also be the quality that rushes up to break out from too much tameness and repetition—too much domestication.

Here is a dream on this matter of wild versus domestic.

I am trying to close the house door, but several lionesses, a single male lion with a huge mane, and a tiger with fur bristling keep banging it open. My domestic cat wants to be with them. I keep trying to separate the domestic cat and bring her indoors and keep the wildcats outdoors. But neither the wildcats nor the domestic cat want to be separated; they want to be free to come inside or go outside at will. I don't feel threatened, only frustrated. They all want to be together and play, but I'm not comfortable with wildcats coming into the house, though they don't really cause much problem once they do push their way in.

I awoke and wondered whether I may be trying too hard to separate domestic and wild natures. Here is the surprise: part of the wild nature of women *is* domestic life, consisting of a home, a family, community, and belonging. The real problem comes from restricting women's behavior and freedom (coming and going from the house). We must let go of controlling the felines' activities.

Some of us know the experience of being gripped by a fantasy. For me, the gripping fantasy was that of being a surf yogini in Central or South America. It began as an urge when I started my doctoral research but became an obsessive desire for a time. The fantasy was idyllic: *I teach yoga, surf, research, and write every day in the sun. My eight-year-old son is with me and goes to an English school. Life is relaxed, fun, and easy. I rent out my house in Canada, and it largely funds living in Nicaragua. Of course, I find a partner to share the experience with.* This fantasy was my idea of perfection. I know women who have embarked on various forms of their gripping fantasies. My fantasy would keep me awake through the wee hours as these thoughts danced in my mind; then I realized that the fantasy was related to this process somehow. I recognized that the fantasy was irrational: I do not speak Spanish; I do not surf well; I am scared of sharks; I like cleanliness; I do not know anyone there, and I would be alone, lonely, and unsupported; and I doubt my son's father would actually let me take our child to Nicaragua so that I could be a surf yogini, nor would I want my son to be away from his father. I had been observing this fantasy and pondering what was at the core of it: Was it a desire to run away from life and escape responsibilities? Or was it a desire to run toward life and not be contained by the smallness of conventional life? What was the inspirator—the pointy-eared, wild woman—saying to me through this fantasy? As I leaned into it more and more, I concluded that—as with the dream of the wildcats and domestic cats—what was required was to hold the tensions and not jump from one side to the other. I was being called on to find a way to incorporate both poles into my life, which during that time was feeling too domestic, responsible, and weighty. I needed to bring in more experiences that were relaxed, fun, and easy.

I have the opportunity to live in intimate engagement with nature. I live in a small town in British Columbia, Canada, named Squamish, which in the local native language means *mother of the wind*. When the pink salmon run from the Pacific and up the rivers, and the blackberries sweeten in August, the ecology teems with creatures. Bears, eagles, coyotes, cougars, bobcats, frogs, and humans all share the same trails and forests. It is a heightened time, because every year brings a confrontation usually involving a domestic pet and a wild animal (often, wildcats). I spend several hours a week in the forest—usually wet, because our coastal town is located in a temperate rain forest. When I started graduate school, hiking became a priority, often undertaken alone. I could take all of me, including my problems, to the granite monolith, the Stawamus Chief mountain, which became my friend by always accepting me—and in that way, the mountain taught me to accept myself. That relationship has shaped and strengthened my body, my psyche, and my work. Connecting with nature is a nourishing practice in a woman's life; it is both sensual and spiritual.

I began studying ecopsychology not knowing what it was, thinking it was perhaps a save-Earth or green movement. Not that I am opposed to such movements, but the enormity of the tasks overwhelms me. Ecopsychology is actually about becoming more natural and authentic; in tending our inner wilds, we indirectly tend Earth, and conversely, extraverts who tend the outer world eventually get led to tend their inner world. Saving self and Earth are not two separate endeavors. Furthermore, unless we dare drop into our own psychic depths (that inner wild) we will continue to perpetuate the purely rational mindset that is largely responsible for environmental destruction in the first place. When you tend the inner, you become more concerned with the outer.

This process of tending the inner wilds is yet another way of describing individuation. Jung described that living consciously is our form of individuation. "A plant that is meant to produce a flower is not individuated if it does not produce it—and the man who does not develop consciousness is not individuated, because consciousness is his flower—it is his life" (Jung, 1976, pp. 296-297). Consciousness is not necessarily the ultimate goal in a human life; nevertheless, it is a rich image of consciousness as a flower that opens and expands to reach its apex of *beauty*. The purpose is so complete in the expanding—while ephemeral in its impermanence. Here is a different suggestion: that life is also in service to beauty for beauty's sake, not necessarily consciousness, though becoming conscious and individuating may happen by being reverent of beauty. Flowering into a conscious, individuated human being can be seen as being in service to beauty. *Conscious* here is not meant in the way of an upward movement, but in the way of getting to know one's self and the archetypes and complexes at work on us. This nurtures an expanded field of relatedness as we come to know who we each uniquely are. Of course, this is ever evolving and never fixed, and so is an ongoing process. *Conscious* is also congruent with Jung's meaning, which is an awareness of the objective psyche or the Self, but we do not want to be identified with that, because it is a force greater than we are; we relate to it as best we can with our ego.

Theodore Roszak (1992) coined the term *ecopsychology* in his book *The Voice of the Earth: An Exploration of Ecopsychology*. It is a distinct field of study that is relevant to this book because it is closely linked to the wild feminine that is ever present in the natural world— same as developing relationship to the wild woman means developing a soulful, embodied life that is liberated or becoming liberated from cultural socialization. Ecopsychology is also a practice of return to a naturalness both within and without in a way that frees us from the conditioning of socialization. Connecting to the natural world enlivens the wild woman and allows her to speak through the symbolic language of nature. The natural world helps us recover our instinctive and intuitive qualities and teaches us how to relate to the young cedar, summer spiders, or the bear. As we enjoy relatedness to the natural world, we are invited into a sense of well-being and a belonging to an animate world where we are all part of nature's dream. When we feel part of nature's dream, we feel connected to something bigger than ourselves, and then we do not have to worry about anything or do anything or be anything; we are just there, and *it*, that is, *life*, is simply happening. However, the wild woman is still dominated by the patriarchy both in women's psyches and in the culture; and ecopsychology writers such as Susan Griffin and Gary Snyder are destabilizing the dominant system. We hear the wild woman in the roar of their work.

Even though Roszak formalized ecopsychology relatively recently, we can recognize the idea of psyche and nature as being indivisible in Jung's early writings and work. According to Jung, psyche and nature are not two separate substances, but are rather one in the same. Our psyche is part of nature and it is enigmatic and limitless, thus we cannot define either the psyche or nature, they are two different aspects of one and the same thing. The wild woman is a personification of the natural psyche in women, and ecopsychology offers a way of relating to her while honoring her as enigmatic.

To define nature, we delve into something mysterious and expansive, where *everything* belongs to nature, including the obvious such as animals, plants, forest, rocks, rivers, and oceans—all things belonging to Earth. But complex ideas fit into this idea of nature as well, including such concepts as the collective unconscious, archetypes, reflection, rationality, and human consciousness. Gary Snyder (1990), in *The Practice of the Wild*, tells us that the inner wilderness included imagination, thoughts, memories, images, angers, and delights. The depths of the mind, the unconscious, are our inner wilderness areas.

All those things are nature. By extension, cities also fit into the definition of nature, though they are neither wild nor part of the wilderness; but they are natural as places of habitat. This is a surprising paradox: women consciously engaging with the wild woman have a proclivity to domesticity as part of their wildish nature; the problems arise when women become dominated and overly socialized or overly domesticated.

In the 70s there was a backlash against this. Susan Griffin (1978) wrote *Woman and Nature: The Roaring Inside Her*, which taps into the repressed feminine voice that wants to roar and uncage women who are too civilized. Griffin uses multiple voices to express the patriarchy that men and women in Western culture are immersed in and uses other voices to express the oppressed feminine. Somewhat unexpectedly, associating woman with nature furthers the oppression of women. First, the assumption in our hierarchical culture implies an elevation of men over both nature and women. "Not only are human beings elevated above the rest of nature, but men are closer to heaven than women. In short, the idea that women are closer to nature is an argument for the dominion of men," articulates Griffin, (p. ix). Through the hierarchical lens of patriarchy, culturally, we have valued ascension and spiritual heights over matter and earthly existence; spiritual heights being represented as heaven, sky father, and transcendent of and superior to earthly existence.

When, in fact, to have the gift of life—in a body with abilities for consciousness, sensation, and relationships—to live on this Earth is such a blessing and such a mystery, why would we hang on to the fantasy that heaven is out there someplace? Heaven is right here. Culturally, we aspire to ascend to heaven in order to engage the fantasy of rising above suffering—and life does include suffering. But it also includes love, joy, beauty, and countless emotions and experiences. We do not have the ability to remember or know a previous life or an afterlife; we have consciousness of only this life. Let us live well while we can. And let us be grateful for the gift of life—making each moment count. Rather than ascending and moving away from life, let us celebrate it here and now. Let us accept our human nature, our finitude, our mortality, and our one life right now. In connecting with the wild woman, we discover a vision of freedom from an imprisoning state of mind. "Liberation from a limiting philosophy, from a habit of self-deception that prevents us from treasuring what we actually possess: life," (Griffin, 1978, p. xi). As we liberate ourselves from patriarchal dominion both individually and collectively we are free to fully appreciate our own unique lives.

Culturally, wild and free have become connected to each other, and for some, those descriptors may inspire the image of galloping carefree across open fields with mane flying in the wind, or of cruising down a long windy highway on a motorbike, or of sipping pretty pink drinks at a palm-fronded beach bar after a day of surfing in a distant land. If considered strictly symbolically, such images reveal the soul's deeper yearning to be wild and free; for example, the desire to be a surf yogini in a distant land may symbolize a yearning to be free of the dominant culture—at least partially. That does not necessarily mean the soul is yearning to be untethered from day-to-day life and responsibilities—child-rearing, cooking, paying the mortgage—but that the soul is yearning to be free of the unconscious autonomous archetypes that dominate. At times, that soul may also need more play, spontaneity, relaxation, or adventure when the day-to-day responsibilities get too much. The feeling generated by the fantasy images of wild and free is perhaps more important than the literalization of the fantasy. The more we come to acknowledge, accept, and appreciate the state of our human condition, with all our individual problems, the more wild and free we are. In alchemy, we free the soul from matter by becoming conscious of the unconscious factors affecting us. We want to become conscious of the patriarchy that dominates women and nature, our inner wilds, and Earth. To be truly free one must take on the basic conditions as they are—painful, impermanent, open, imperfect—and then be grateful for the impermanence, and the freedom it grants us. In a fixed universe, there would be no freedom. "With that freedom we improve the campsite, teach children, oust tyrants," says Snyder (1990).

The world is nature and, in the long run, inevitably wild, because wild, as the process and essence of nature, is also an ordering of impermanence.

We can define the term *wild* with great care, first the Oxford dictionary definition: "uncivilized, rude, resisting constituted government, unrestrained, licentious, dissolute, insubordinate, violent, destructive, cruel, unruly." We can interpret the inverse of the meaning as Snyder suggests. Societies whose economic system is in a close and sustainable relation to the local ecosystem; following local custom, style, and etiquette without concern for the standards of the metropolis; unintimidated, self-reliant, independent, fiercely resisting any oppression, confinement, or exploitation; expressive, physical, openly sexual, ecstatic. When we look at the term *wild* through the lens of the oppressor, our own patriarchal dominant, then the word connotes something threatening because control and order will be upturned. However, if we look at it through the lens of the wild woman, then the word suddenly becomes liberating and respectful of self and other. We can see how that becomes a needed and powerful lens in the context of national politics which so strongly influence society and culture; and yet democracies are intended to represent the people. Doing the individual work of individuation becomes essential to creating a healthy, balanced collective.

Who is a woman before she is socialized? What would a wild woman really do and what would she be like? What is the pure form of the wild woman? We are shaped by society, or as Simone de Beauvoir in her 1949 treatise *The Second Sex* wrote, 'One is not born, but rather becomes, a woman.' Recall those stories of boy children being found in the wild, raised by wolves. What would a girl child be like? I think of María, the Shipibo shaman woman, nearly a hundred years old, born and raised in a tribal village in the Amazon. She does not know anything about my energy-efficient home with its modern, open floor plan, red kitchen, gas fireplace, and large windows. How strange this Western way seems.

Peaks and Vales

Spirit and soul get conflated often, but they are different terms and have distinct meanings. Let us differentiate spirit and psyche (soul) by drawing on Hillman's (2005) essay "Peaks and Vales: The Soul/Spirit Distinction as Basis for the Differences Between Psychotherapy and Spiritual Discipline." Soul we see in our fantasy images. That is how the psyche presents itself directly. That is her language. All consciousness depends upon fantasy images. Soul is expressed through fantasy, images, and symbolic language. Spirit on the other hand is expressed as heights and peak experiences, "the clamber up the peaks in search of spirit is the drive of the spirit in search of itself," in search of our own God-likeness and an experience of God-nearness. Soul, on the other hand, belongs down in the vales such as depressed emotional places, vales of tears, a long depression or hollow. The 14th Dalai Lama describes the difference:

> Soul is at home in the deep, shaded valleys. Heavy torpid flowers saturated with black growth. The rivers flow like warm syrup. They empty into huge oceans of soul. Spirit is a land of high, white peaks and glittering jewel-like lakes and flowers. Life is sparse and sounds travel great distances. There is soul music, soul food, soul dancing, and soul love. (Hillman, 2005, pp. 76-77)

The journey to reclaim the wild woman is downward into the vales, not upward, and there is an urgency to re-inhabit the matter of our bodies and lives.

After my divorce, I took an ascetic path, denying all pleasures. Part of that ascetic practice involved becoming conscious of desires and burning off sulfuric compulsions. However, it became more like repression, and things naturally burst forth out of the shadow in rather messy ways. In hindsight, I was more likely unconsciously trying to ascend and flee the pain of betrayal and the loss of the marriage fantasy of security and wholeness. Perhaps also I was looking for my own spirit.

Or perhaps it was the familiar desire to escape earthly life and all troubles that it brings—illness, suffering, need for food/money. There is a mistaken notion that we must *center ourselves* or *find balance*, but the ideal is to arrive at a place of acceptance of the earthly life as an aspect of the spiritual journey. After a few years on that ascetic path, when I was about to commit to it as a life path, I had a series of dreams depicting a rapid descent to Earth—like Icarus falling from the sky and into the ocean after traveling too close to the sun—only unlike Icarus, I did not die. The ocean always broke my fall, and I could swim to shore. There was another dream of going through a portal with an animus figure and "back to the full range of human feeling and emotion" and another of an animus figure resuscitating me by breathing pneuma (spirit) into my body. I followed the guidance and left the ascetic path to find my way back to my own instinctual body, to matter, and mater, the original maternal ground—Earth's oceanic amniotic fluid. These were the early stages of discovering the repressed feminine, the wild woman.

I was simultaneously discovering the animus as psychopomp between the conscious and unconscious worlds both inwardly and outwardly as a projection and a lived relationship with the wild, bear-man with whom I was falling in love. The anima was also developing; however, I was initially more conscious of the animus aspect through dreams, active imaginations, lived experience, and ceremonial visions. This archetype of the anima/animus also presents as a single shape-shifter—from man-woman-man-woman personifications—and can also be theriomorphic, sometimes in the same figure as a man-woman shape-shifter. I differentiate anima and animus for this book, though I do so lightly and fluidly, being careful to not literalize or make this definition of dual, psychic sexes fixed, because I imagine it as both two separate aspects and one single aspect. This is only one fantasy, and there are many ways to imagine this mysterious guide.

The anima—the feminine in women—must develop, and externally, women begin to find their way when they find relationship to other women. This is a turning point in our journey of finding a new vision. Women have to develop deeply authentic relationships with women as we develop our relationship to the inner feminine, the wild woman. At my house some evenings, women gather over wine, cheese, grapes, and pastries; and we talk of women's issues. We resurrect the women's mysteries in our deep talks about child-rearing, menstruation, orgasms, husbands, lovers, divorce, affairs, loneliness, restlessness, daydreams, nightdreams, fantasies, art, hopes, despair, depression, aching, longing, medicinal plants, yoga, prayer, forests, bears, cougars, surfing, aliens, tarot, the moon, crop circles, and growing our own food. We come up with new possibilities, ideas, and perspectives. We accept and we listen. In the telling and listening, we love and support. We hear and see each other and ourselves; we see ourselves in each other. I am grateful for the sisterhood. Some nights we even try on each other's high heels. Occasionally, we even go out dressed up wearing heels because we enjoy feeling like sexy women. We celebrate sexuality and beauty and Aphrodite. We speak of what we know: that the light is within us.

A New Paradigm

It is an important time as this new vision emerges. Christianity has dominated the past age in the Western world, and we are now at the time of the birthing of a new paradigm. We are in an in-between time: leaving behind the mythology of a one and only God who has fled while we wait for the God who is coming. In fact, the new paradigm may not be a God who is coming at all. We are at a time of great transition; we must save the phenomena of angels, images, gods and things themselves; we also must allow new phenomena—such as the embodied wild woman—to emerge; and we want to leave room for mystery to unfold. The world is at a critical time in its great history, and we humans have, for the first time, a lot of power over what will happen because of our choices and actions. This time of change that we are in is captured in what the Greeks called the *kairos*—the right moment— for a "metamorphosis of the gods," of the fundamental principles and symbols. This peculiarity of our time, which is certainly not of our conscious choosing, is the expression of the unconscious within us who is changing. We are at a moment in time for a new paradigm, and it is not of our conscious choosing; it seems impelled by a force greater than we are, and yet we seem to have the power to co-create with it.

We can wonder why *this* time? Why the pervasive masculinity of Western intellectual and spiritual tradition has suddenly become so apparent to us today, whereas it remained invisible to almost every previous generation? Richard Tarnas (1991), in *The Passion of the Western Mind: Understanding the Ideas That Have Shaped Our World View*, suggests we are experiencing something that looks very much like the death of modern man, indeed that looks very much like the death of the Western man. Perhaps the end of man himself is at hand. "But man is not a goal. Man is something that must be overcome—and fulfilled, in the embrace of the feminine" (p. 445). There is a resurgence that has been emerging for many years, but culturally, it is a relatively new phenomenon. The experience of the archetypal feminine affects both men and women individually as well as at the collective cultural level. As women, we want reintegration of the feminine at the personal level; however, reintegration also has larger cultural implications as individuals come into relationship with the wild woman. The reintegration of the repressed feminine and the necessity for the masculine to undergo an ego death could shatter its most established beliefs about itself and the world. Perhaps this is why we see a strong neo-conservative political backlash. Despite that backlash, a threshold must now be crossed, a threshold demanding a courageous act of faith, of imagination, of trust in a larger and more complex reality; a threshold, moreover, demanding an act of unflinching self-discernment. We find the courage to become more self-aware and integrate the feminine in order to move into a time of something radically new and uncertain. We cannot remember a time when Western culture was inclusive and not repressive of the feminine.

The dominant power, however, is not going to relinquish supremacy easily. We are witnessing a huge counter-response to the emergence of the feminine. This is seen in the force of today's political and religious arenas. How will the wild woman respond? She is coming, like it or not. If individuals and the culture at large fight and resist the wild woman's presence, there will be fear, suffering, and struggle. However, if we can meet her open heartedly, with gratitude for the new beginning that she offers us, and if we can host her as a welcomed guest, then we can receive her greatest gift: her love. But it takes time to build trust, and we will have to patiently endure times when the ego reverts to old patterns. That, however, does not imply apathy. We must allow her to roar.

We do not yet know what this new cosmology will look like. In addition to Jung, Avens, and Tarnas, James Hillman (2007a) also wrote about a new cosmology. In *Mythic Figures*, he kept the context to a critique of analytic psychology's being stuck in the Oedipus myth; however, his critique can apply to anyone seeking wisdom and self-knowledge. In fact, it can apply to the whole of the Western paradigm. Hillman argued that psychotherapy was still in the Oedipus myth—the same way our quest is for the truth about ourselves and for self-knowledge. He tried to find another road by looking to Dionysus, Hades, to a post-Apollonian consciousness, and, earlier, to Psyche and Eros (in *The Myth of Analysis*, 1972)—only to conclude that we are still enrapt in the Oedipal fantasy and that a psychology of anima released from the tyranny of Oedipus is still not possible. The new myth involves the liberation of the feminine from patriarchal dominion. We are collectively searching and moving into a new cosmology where beauty and love *can* be at the center. We can feel Hillman's frustrated urgency in his words.

> Where is beauty in psychology—in its theories, in its training of psychologists, in the language it speaks and writes, in the dress of its practitioners? The disregard of display insults Aphrodite and narrows the idea of soul to only the unseen interior of human beings. Psychology goes about its business of exploring the human heart ignoring that heart's essential longing—not only for love, but for beauty. (2007a, p. 18)

We each have the choice to open our hearts and greet the cosmology from a place of love, or we can cling to certainty and meet the world from a place of fear.

As we offer our intention, attention, and presence to beauty—to love—we will move into a myth that is attuned to the beauty of our day-to-day lives. We can appreciate in the moment the strawberries and crocuses that arise in the spring, the fresh snow on mountaintops, the moistness of rich soil, the smile of a child, the gaze of a beloved, the warmth of a fire, the richness of wine, the fullness of our breath, and so on. We engage in life in a sensual, embodied way. Rumi (1995) wrote: "Let the beauty we love be what we do. There are hundreds of ways to kneel and kiss the ground" (p. 36). That idea celebrates both beauty and love as among the highest values—values that belong to the wild woman—as well as to Aphrodite.

In my own imagining, spirit and matter intersect at the heart chakra as the point of soulfulness. To reclaim the feminine is to embody expression and live from the heart, and it involves nothing less than the willingness to suffer the path of self-knowledge. We must recognize and honor our originality, passion, vision, and an ethical commitment to living what we know. Ensouling our bodies in this way will redeem the oppressed voice and body of the wild woman, liberating her shadowy and distorted forms into a joyful resonance, and sing back to the cosmos a darker, mysterious whole.

One of the challenges in following the heart path is loneliness. It is a surprise that the heart path—the path of love and relatedness—could be a lonely path, but it requires that one reconsider the collective and maybe leave the sanctioned paradigm in favor of one's own path. The experience of loneliness is a part of the individuation process. It can be difficult to meet other people who accept the oddness of some of our decisions and difficult to find people who do not judge, who are walking their *own* paths and living what *they* know. It is enough to be with our own self-doubts, fears, judgments, and uncertainties about what we are doing; but to have to contend with naysayers makes it even more challenging. Thus, the loneliness.

Culturally, we have clear ideas about which behaviors are acceptable and which ones are not. Clarity is valued over chaos, boundaries over blurriness, monogamy over polygamy, fidelity over infidelity, certainty over uncertainty, knowable over unknowable, and so on. However, soul seems to have other ideas: a woman's heart may well go on of its own volition; our rational mind influences our actions, but not our feelings. Choosing *simplicity* seems to be more about just accepting what soul is drawn to rather than resisting it, but that does not necessarily mean acting on it. In fact, holding the tension between opposites is often what is required. Breaking the tension can require a period of starting over, holding the opposites in tension again until they build up energy, and, hopefully, holding the tension longer each time—until, eventually, a new way arises and/or the problem is simply outgrown; such is the transcendent function introduced by Jung (1929/1969). If we recognize we are in a psychological death/rebirth cycle, we must not thwart the death cycle and then become annoyed when rebirth does not follow immediately. If we thwart the death cycle by breaking the tension—replaying the pattern—and then have to start over again, the rebirth cannot come. That can go on for years and can destroy lives. We must allow the symbolic death (such as the end of a relationship); and when it comes time to let it go, we have to let it go and then venture bravely into the unknown, where the new life is waiting.

Let us have a closer look at the transcendent function. This is one of Jung's foundational concepts and is important experientially as the wild woman emerges because she creates conflict with the old, conscious attitude. It is a gestation period for the as-yet unconscious idea, attitude, or archetype that wants to be born into consciousness; it incubates until the time is right. Sometimes the problem that is causing the tension is simply outgrown with time; at other times, a third image emerges that reconciles and integrates the two poles. There is a period of laying the groundwork that takes discipline to prepare—like an athlete who trains and learns the skills and then, letting go, surrenders into the flow or the zone.

The tension of opposites can be identified whenever a conflict arises. Two things will be in opposition to each other, in tension, and the job of the conscious ego is to hold that tension and stay present with it. As long as we hold that tension, we are preparing the groundwork for the transcendent attitude to arise out of the unconscious. The intensity can get extreme, and the ego requires discipline and patience to persist with the process until the third thing, the new symbol, emerges. The transcendent function arises from the union of conscious and unconscious contents. It is called transcendent because it makes the transition from one attitude to another organically possible state, one that transcends the various pairs of opposites. If we are patient and can endure the pressures without being reactive and falling back into the old mode or unconscious state, it has the potential to create a solution between heart and mind.

Artemis

It feels risky to suggest that Aphrodite, Greek goddess of beauty and love, could be at the center of a new cosmology—risky because I would hate to offend Artemis, who is significant to the wild woman. The Greek goddess Artemis, whose name means "bear," embodies the wisdom of the wild. The wild woman archetype is the complete feminine in all her expressions; as such, both Artemis and Aphrodite are personifications of two different aspects of that archetype. In this imagining—that the wild woman is both one and many representations of the feminine—we can differentiate her personifications and aspects and relate to them separately without being exclusionary. From this perspective, we can examine Artemis more closely and not get impeded by the incompatibility of Artemisian consciousness and Aphroditic consciousness. The virgin (one in herself) goddess Artemis is the archetype of a femininity that is pure and primitive. Hers is an absolute femininity that is not defined by a relationship to a lover, child, father, or husband; in other words, Artemis is not defined by any reality of the masculine world. Artemis too is very beautiful—some say as beautiful as Aphrodite; however, this beauty is not for the benefit of any reproductive union, this beauty exists for itself.

Interlude:

This section on Artemis is hard to write. Why can't she just have a single beloved and put me out of my misery from trying to figure this out? Why must she be chaste from men? Why is it so important to have a companion? Is Artemis different from the wild woman? I know something other than my ego is guiding this work, because "I" for certain do not know what "I'll" write next. Wild Woman, I call upon your help now.

"There is a place in you that must be preserved and protected like the virgin forest. It must be fought for. So many trees have fallen. The Peregrines, endangered, abandon their chicks in the nest because of nearby logging and blasting. The bear gets shot because she knocks over garbage cans to feed her cub. The cougar, shot, because she aggressed cyclists too close to where she was feeding on her deer. And on. You know this place in nature. You know this place within you—the place that has not always been tended as a sacred grove, but has known violation, conquest, and irreverence. I, Artemis, am defender of the sacred grove. No more disrespect to these lands. There is no room for man to come with anything but reverence to this deep forest."

(Sigh). Thank you, Artemis.

End interlude.

I included the preceding transference dialogue because it was spontaneous and authentic to my struggle, and because of that, it seemed to cut through cleanly to a deeper, autonomous wisdom.

Ginette Paris's work fleshes out these ideas around the importance of recovering Artemisian consciousness in women.

> I believe indeed that the loss of a Goddess so fiercely opposed to all contact with the opposite sex, but nevertheless adored and respected by all, has meant a loss for all women of their power to defend a sacred territory, interior and exterior, physical or psychic. Nature, flora and fauna, is universally exploitable and commercializable, and since women are associated with nature, they have also become touchable, violable, and utilizable. (1986, p. 115)

This returns to the earlier argument that it is not favorable to see woman as closer to nature than man, because it disempowers both women and nature. We want to recognize we are—*all* of us, *each* of us— nature. We can see that Artemis is the fierce protector of a mysterious core of an untouchable femininity in women and in nature and that that core must remain virginal. Women must claim the art of preserving within themselves a force that is intact, inviolable, and radically feminine. An Artemisian nature is available to all of us that can guard and protect the untamable primitive femininity.

Artemis frequently dominates me: maybe this is my disposition, maybe because I am an only child, maybe because it is hard for me to trust men, maybe because I just like bears and nature. Who knows? However, with Artemis, there is a fear that I will be solitary the rest of my life, and because I am only at midlife and desirous of having passions in my future, such fear puts me in conflict with Artemis's protection. Those of us who have recovered the wild woman will not lose ourselves again, but for those of us still unpartnered, most of us do hope to have a relationship—and women are finding men who can be in relationship to a feminine woman who belongs to herself.

For those of us who are predominantly introverted, as opposed to extroverted, we not only *enjoy* alone time; we need it, or we become overwhelmed and snappy. Aloneness is essential to introverts' well-being, but too much aloneness can become frightening too. Fear of Artemis is connected to a fear of radical solitude and of unprotected confrontation with self. Artemis is the one who calls us into our Self and our solitude. She is the one who calls us into the liminal space of the transitional rebirth. At midlife, this rebirthing of one's self and one's life is often painful and difficult when Artemis is the midwife. But we all have a responsibility to answer to the call of the goddess and sit with her and our uncomfortable emotions as we go through the rebirth process.

In a woman's life, the counterbalance to an overly dominant patriarchal culture may for a time involve the pendulum swinging toward Artemis. Artemisian consciousness, the absolute feminine that is defined by her absence of patriarchal dominance, is more important than ever as a corrective to a culture that is rebirthing itself. However, facing that goddess is not without potential peril: "There is a risk in Artemis's world of losing one's capacity for human communication, danger in being caught helplessly within one's anima-lity" (Downing, 1981, p. 168). We can get too embedded in the world of Artemis and too far from relating to other humans. I recognize that tendency in myself when, despite my loneliness and longing, I prefer to be alone for prolonged periods rather than engaging with others; or other introverted women will engage in meditation, or in novels, or with animals rather than in human relatedness.

The time of rebirth is the time of Artemis; and it can be a long labor. My own reemergence took almost a decade, and five of those years were hard labor—though most women I encounter personally and professionally in my clinical practice do not seem to require such a long awakening period. Following times of great aloneness, we can be grateful for the newfound company of wizened wild women who magically appear and propagate in our lives. As for male companionship, there continued a longer period of aloneness, and the only one who was not *slayed* by Artemis—she who slays—was the one like Orion, the wild bear-man, who could maintain platonic though intimate friendship; any other man was slayed by Artemis's unfailing arrow that would seem to come out of nowhere.

There was a dream while writing this section on Artemis.

I am a student buying books in a grocery store. The cashier is a black woman, and she is so agonizingly slow that I miss one of my classes. An older black woman stands so close behind me that she is breathing down my neck. I playfully say to her, "Only my boyfriend stands this close; do you mind making more room for me." She backs up and we engage in playful banter while we wait in the short but slow line. Finally, at the cashier, I make another playful comment about the delay and about my books, one of them on women's sexuality. The cashier returns the light banter. She tells me there is a problem with my credit card.

I hurry back to my dorm room minutes before the next class starts, wearing high heels (elevated status perhaps? also sexy, the way Aphrodite would approve of). I walk with grace and ease that surprise me. At my dormitory door, I am flustered and feel overwhelmed, my patience has run out, and I need alone time to recompose myself and change my clothes to something more comfortable. A woman meets me at my door and is pestering me about where my husband is. "Isn't this his room? Isn't he in there? Aren't you his wife?" she asks. I'm annoyed at this woman looking for my husband; I don't have a husband. "No, I'm just me—Stacey. I don't have a husband." I am really rattled now. I just want to be alone, but I have only six minutes to get to my next class.

Dreams often speak to us about what is happening in our lives at that present time. At that time, I was enjoying a deeply satisfying relationship with the oppressed feminine that was emerging (the black women), but it was also delaying me from my next class. I have

61

concerns about my finances and my earning ability with this newfound feminine consciousness, because I have no intention of or interest in again reengaging in a patriarchal workforce or a corporate life. I wonder: who is the absent, but pervasively felt, figure in the dream (and in me) that undervalues and oppresses the feminine so that "I" do not get the credit I deserve? I have an appreciation of Aphrodite's sexy heels and, in the dream, the desire to allure a particular like-minded man— hoping to be seen and noticed. I am annoyed at this part of me (Hera perhaps?) that is looking for "my husband." There is no husband. I need to be alone. My comfortable place is always in Artemisian retreat, in solitude. I do feel an urgency to get somewhere important quickly; there is not much time for aloneness right now. This woman who annoys and overwhelms me, the one looking for my husband, is the one I decide to move toward imaginally because she evokes the most significant affect: annoyance.

I dialogued with her in my journal and became even more frustrated and annoyed as she revealed to me both the depth of my longing for a secure attachment with a male and my utter inability to create it. I am ashamed of my longing for a relationship, as though I were weak and insecure for wanting it. I feel a false pride in my identification with Artemis: that I-do-not-need-a-man attitude. I have goals involving school and woman friends and my son and my home and my garden and hiking and yoga all to fill me up. I feel angry with this woman who wants a relationship so badly, as though I were incomplete without it. I am *so* utterly complete unto myself that I actually do need a man in order to truly experience vulnerability in intimacy. I cannot change my singleness by will; I can only look at it and accept it and experience other ways of being vulnerable, such as creativity.

She who seeks *my husband* asks what I would choose at the end of my life: to have had more education, more work, or more romantic love. At the time, I feel angry with her; love, of course. The frustration comes from feeling disempowered to manifest it. I am at the mercy of the goddesses. "Would you even *merge* with another?" Merge: this is Aphrodite's realm. My vision has been of finding a romantic love where

"I" would remain "I," and the "other" would remain "other." Merge? It is humbling to know how fiercely I protect my sovereignty in true Artemisian fashion.

A great deal of difficulty attends the relationship between Artemis and Aphrodite. Part of the attraction of Artemis is pathological, inspired by a fear of intimacy and commitment, of losing myself in *that* way. Whereas Aphrodite will come to help against Artemis and seems to appear to lure me away from self and towards another. The fear of merging with another is the same fear of losing myself in *that* way. With the few men I am drawn to, I complain that they are afraid of intimacy and commitment, which is nothing other than a mirror for my own fear. In fact, my preoccupation with the shadow feminine that keeps me from getting to "my next class" may well be another distraction from intimacy. The woman of my dream showed me just how intense my fear is, based on my anger when she asked me if I would merge. Some women notice the entwinement between the call to solitude and the recall to relationship. Yet for many of us who have been single mothers for many years, it is a challenge to trust the eventual return of Aphrodite; in fact, after such a prolonged period of aloneness, I feel angry at her unfulfilled promises of love. Artemis and solitude, on the other hand, have always been there and are trustworthy at least.

This exploration prompted another dream:

From outside looking in, I watch a bear go into my bedroom through an open window. It was not much of a problem that the bear was taking up residency in my bedroom, so long as the window remained open for it to come and go at will and not feel caged or enclosed. Then the dream jumped to arousing and erotic coupling with a woman, with "me" as a man (though I also simultaneously felt I was both the subject and the object—the man and the woman—and there was something about the "objectification" of the woman). Then it jumped again to me as a woman wearing high heels at a campsite.

I awoke with the feeling that wild women, bear women, enjoy wild sexuality. I thought of Engel's (2009) novel *Bear* and the heroine's sexual relationship with a bear that ultimately liberates her sexuality. I welcome the bear into my bedroom. Wildness and sexuality need not, maybe even *should* not, be separated. We want to keep the window open for the bear to come and go; it may be drafty, but after all, bear hugs are warm.

Re-View

Here we look over what we found in this chapter—we review, view again, but from a new perspective. We evoked the wild woman and expressed her essence without capturing and confining her as an ever-dynamic archetypal presence. We have drawn upon both a knowing that is clear and of the mind and a knowing that is obscure and of the soul in order to honor the fullness of her complexity. We worked at defining her, and we moved into ecopsychology to deepen our understanding of the wild woman. We explored the significance of the reemergence of the feminine both individually and collectively in order to ground the importance of that archetype as we collectively co-create a new cosmology that values and honors the feminine. It is a time that we give birth to a new paradigm on every level, and the wild woman archetype shall be an intrinsic aspect of the rebirth. We explored Artemis, the goddess of the rebirth and addressed the importance of differentiating the many faces of the wild woman. As women, when we differentiate the faces of the wild woman we then become more liberated to explore other issues that are important to us, such as psychological development, relationships, and sexuality, each of which is examined in subsequent chapters.

CHAPTER 3
Women's Psychological Development

Tell me for what you yearn and I shall tell you who you are.
We are what we reach for, the idealized image that drives
our wandering.

Hillman, 1989, pp. 53-54

The complexity and common themes of women's psychological development at midlife is vast. Let us examine this topic while confining our efforts to areas that seem to support the development of the wild woman archetype. We first explore previous relevant literature. We further excavate the Jungian concept of individuation and specifically, the sacred aspect and role of suffering in the process. *Individuation* for this purpose is the overarching term that encompasses women's psychological development. We examine and critique parts of the myth of Psyche and Eros as a guide to women's individuation and consider how the myth may be evolving for embodied wild women. There is a section each on the masculine aspect and the feminine aspect, though we limit the highly-differentiated personifications of the gods and goddesses. Differentiation of those energies is important, even essential; however, we are looking at the larger shift occurring in women by addressing the all-encompassing energies imagined here as *masculine* and *feminine* qualities.

Masculine energies or qualities include activity, dominance, sun, clarity, polarity, spirit, idealism, individuality, ascent, either-or, and linear. Feminine principles include passivity, submission, moon, mystery, holism, body, practicality, relationship, descent, both-and, and cyclical. Both men and women have both masculine and feminine qualities, but most of us initially have more masculine qualities by nature of socialization in a patriarchal culture. We are part of a time in which the feminine principle is emerging in both men and women—in women this most frequently occurs after midlife. For women to be *wild* and *free* to express the emergent wild woman, our psychologies mature until we become able to liberate ourselves from the old paradigms that entangle us. There is a story about a whale that cannot know water until it has been on the beach. It is arduous to become aware of the water we swim in, and even then, we can never know the whole ocean. This is equivalent to uncomfortably gaining objectivity so as to become aware of the patriarchal culture we live in.

Before beginning the drafting of this chapter, I had an intense compulsion to wander off, with no fixed agenda. I was able to set aside time in early November to yield to that pull: I got in my car and headed south for a long weekend. I kept wondering about the opening quote by Hillman (1989): "Tell me for what you yearn and I shall tell you who you are. We are what we reach for, the idealized image that drives our wandering." What do I yearn for? I kept hearing certain words that came from a dream I had had about six months earlier: "She wanders into the world until she is lost, then she becomes the world." This speaks about the unification and presence that come when the ego lets go of trying to control everything. I yearn to feel that connection. I yearn for love. I yearn for soulfulness and spiritual experience. I yearn to know that the gods and goddesses are not ambivalent. I yearn to know that the deities love me. "How can I *know* such a thing?" I wonder. I fear their seeming ambivalence, which at times has caused me great suffering. I have even asserted that the archetypes are ambivalent. Those thoughts and words dance around over many highway miles in northwestern Washington.

I eventually found my way to the magical little native village of La Push on the outer coast of the Olympic Peninsula. I strolled the beach, kicking my knee-high rubber boots through the dense seafoam and thinking of Aphrodite's birth. A surprise wave chased me until it tickled my boot tops and my knees with seafoam—I burst into laughter. "Never turn your back on the ocean," was one of the lessons I had been taught as a neophyte surfer; she is always full of surprises. That night a fine Pacific storm howled in. I was cozied up with tea and wool socks, reading Marion Woodman's (1993) *Conscious Femininity*, enthralled by her ideas about the body as the material vessel for the spirit and about the intricacy of the body and soul relationship. Then, from the blackness outside my window, an owl called incessantly. I could not imagine a more perfect moment of feeling the presence of the wild woman archetype. The ocean waves, the storm winds and rain, and then an owl! She beckoned me onto the dark, wet porch, where I perched, wrapped in a blanket, and listened, alert, until I felt I was part of the immediacy of the world I inhabited. I was present with the wild woman in her vastness. I had *become the world* for a moment. Wrapped, and rapt, by this dark femininity, I *knew* I was held and received; I had an embodied knowing that she was not ambivalent to me, and I was flooded full with gratitude and beauty, a reciprocal feeling that might best be called love and included the sensuous connection of Eros.

That night, November 2, All Souls' Day, I had a dream.

> *I was in a school auditorium on a reprieve because it was a special day. A male, perhaps a teacher, handed me his flask— a curvaceous silver embossed vessel that hinged open to reveal two glass flasks inside that fit perfectly side by side. Each was half full of golden "spirits." The man had the main bottles and could top up the glass flasks when needed. The outer flask was unique and had been acquired long before during his travels in Paris. Then a woman dream teacher brought a casket, which she opened to release an inflated old ghost (like a gigantic blow-up-doll balloon). It drifted up to the cathedral ceiling and on and away, gone forever.*

The dream was more lengthy and complex, but I tended the dream beginning with that flask because it enamored me. I drew it and thought of the outer flask as the body that contained the masculine and feminine spirits inside it. I saw the outer flask as the alchemical vessel that contained two clear-glass flasks of nearly equal parts of spiritual ambrosia. It seemed that a spiritual *coniunctio* had occurred within the vessel containing those two smaller flasks.

.   My initial reflection was that the body was the alchemical vessel that hosts the anima and animus; further reflection caused me to consider that the symbolic vessel can also be a relationship between two people. To confirm that pondering, a couple days later—and without her knowing about this dream—I received a personal communication from Betsy Perluss:

> I believe that it is within relationship that we encounter the "old ghosts." Relationship is the alchemical vase. Relationship—and the questions and struggles it brings—is always shape-shifting, asking us to respond, again and again, to each uncertain moment. (B. Perluss, personal communication, 2013)

I realized I had been holding on to a perfectionist ideal: *if I do my work and heal my old wounds, then I will be able to create a perfect, healthy relationship.* Many of us hold on to a moralistic fantasy of perfection—that someday, when we are healed and therefore perfect, we will have the perfect relationship. It is the kind of thinking that belongs to the dualism of the inner patriarch: that there is a *perfect* or *right* way. In that thinking, *healing* implies being in an optimal state and free of suffering. We can commonly operate from the ideal that if we can be healed, we can be rewarded with a relationship free of suffering. The perfection of the human condition necessarily includes the wounds and so-called imperfections; these never fully go away, nor should they, though they may transform as we relate to our wounds. We are perfect as we are, with our so-called imperfections and all. The relationship itself is the vessel—it is not the goal, or the gold, or the lapis—but it is the container that holds the spirits in their transformation process. That idea of relationship as container is so important to this work that I have devoted a separate chapter to it; however, it is inextricable from the process of women's psychological development, and so it overlaps.

From this perspective, my research question could be reversed, in that relationship and sexuality represent the stimulus for reclaiming the wild woman. The question was originally formulated as follows: *What are some of the ways a woman who has recovered the wild woman archetype expresses her sexuality and engages in relationships?* However, it could be reorganized: *What are some of the ways sexuality and relationships inspire a woman to recover the wild woman archetype?* Both of these perspectives are relevant depending on a woman's relationship to the wild woman. This reversibility indicates that perhaps the process is not as linear as we might assume or prefer. The important part of the process is that the wild woman be brought into consciousness, because in most of us, she is in the domain of the shadow. Simultaneously, we must strive to get some perspective from the *beach,* or the waters in which we are swimming while we allow a supportive relationship with the masculine to develop. We are not to discard the body as vessel, either: the image of the two spirit flasks within the unique silver flask is a potent symbol on both the personal level and the lived external level; the two are, ultimately, inseparable.

The body/soul split can occur out of the intellectualizing of a problem that abandons the ensouled body and strives for an idealized perfection and purity. "The soul, like gold, if too refined or pure becomes soft and will not hold its shape. It needs to contain an impurity so that it can harden into an identifiable form" (Woodman, 1982, p. 77). In the pursuit of the alchemical gold, that affirms that the transformer is the impurity: that aspect we each have and that we want to move away from and reject in ourselves—the wounding or place of inferiority. The thing we reject is the thing we must move towards. The addiction to perfection is an addiction to unreality which leaves little room for the feminine. Our striving for perfection kills love because perfection does not recognize humanity. Woodman writes about a woman's addiction to perfection in *doing* rather than *being*, but that once she gives herself over to her love of dancing, painting, and singing, joy is not experienced as selfish or luxurious, but as an absolute need. Women are learning not to be someone else's image but to *be* and express from our own authentic femininity.

There is a risk that this last notion could imply that if we just dance, paint, and sing, then we experience joy, with the further implication that we transcend suffering. Yes, we need to express our creative being, but out of a desire to express ourselves freely, not out of a desire to transcend suffering. The transcendence of suffering is simply not achievable; life would become static. Our addiction to the unreality of perfection is part of our culture's current obsession with self-help *strategies* that are actually more harmful than helpful. Self-help feels anti-wild. The wild woman is about being an embodied human— perfectly imperfect, engaged in each moment of life and not striving to transcend suffering but willing to be transformed by it.

Initial View

The chapter of women's psychological development contains many subcategories: the Self; anima woman; animus as guide; anima-animus as shape-shifter; possession and possessiveness; transference and countertransference; and personalizing, personification, and personifying. The scope of the subcategories is vast and will require limitations of the texts we can scan or scour for guidance.

Even though we moved away from the archetype of the wild virgin, we will still look into Harding's (1971) *Women's Mysteries*. In addition to defining *virgin*—"as a virgin, however, she belonged to herself alone, she was 'one-in-herself'" (p. 79)—Harding discusses how the uprush of feminine instinct in a woman may be like a flooding from the unconscious. Women beginning to experience the wild woman may have dreams of tidal waves and floods during times of crisis such as separating from a marriage and moving toward independence in a way different from that which was experienced prior to marriage.

We have already been looking at the two virgin Greek goddesses Artemis and Aphrodite as presented in Ginette Paris's (1986) book *Pagan Meditations: The Worlds of Aphrodite, Artemis, and Hestia*. Aphrodite and Artemis have very different ways of being self-possessed and virginal: Artemis largely separates herself from the human world, whereas Aphrodite is involved in the union of two but is herself not possessed by any one man. Those two virgin goddesses are pertinent because for us women who have been part of the dominant paradigm and are now accessing the wild woman, they may be at odds with our most-compelling present needs.

In *The Goddess: Mythological Images of the Feminine*, Christine Downing (1981) wrote a beautiful address to Aphrodite. Downing acknowledges Aphrodite's powerful presence in her life in her many guises, including passionate love, her feeling way of being in the world, and love for love's sake and not for progeny. She vulnerably tries to differentiate herself from this powerful goddess and looks at the shadow of Aphrodite—in particular, Aphrodite's sadness in response to lost love. Aphroditic love, after all, is a fleeting love, a love that departs. Downing describes Aphrodite's mode of consciousness as that of the present moment: "you teach the moment, this moment, not the last one or the next" (p. 211). That separation from Aphrodite and from the other is a work of mourning. There is no way to experience Aphrodite's consciousness without also experiencing the inevitable departure. How much time have we spent longing to return to the magic of an Aphroditic encounter or feeling confused by her departure?

Downing's work is around differentiating herself from this goddess; our work is perhaps the same, eventually, but first, we must reacquaint ourselves with her. Downing wrote, "You [Aphrodite] teach us to let go of the illusions of growth and development" (p. 211). In the myth of Cupid and Psyche as told by Apuleius in *The Golden Ass* (written about 160 CE, 1998), Psyche does become conscious, but that is not her goal. Love is her goal: in the form of reunion with Eros. This is an important distinction of that mode of consciousness—particularly in the field of depth psychology, where it can be common to pursue a desire for expanded self-consciousness. Some of us experience love as the catalyst for our awakening, and this is related to Aphrodite.

Those of us who have had Aphrodite and all her charms in shadow for a long time have a hard time trusting her and trusting ourselves with her when she does show up. Sometimes it is hard to resist her sexual passions, when probably there are times it is better if we do not succumb to the alchemical sulfuric element of our desires. She has been ruthless to me at times. It took a long time for me to let go of my marriage, even though my husband had moved on. A marriage ending can be so complicated and full of subtext that we may never fully understand, and in my case, Aphrodite was involved. It can be easy to blame each other based on our pain, yet blame is so destructive to both parties. During the time my marriage was ending, I was thinking it was a result of my husband's actions. Later, however, I realized—though I value family—that I did not want to be married any longer. I felt I had lost myself and was unable to reclaim myself within the dynamic of marriage. Perhaps in this way, Aphrodite's ruthlessness was also a gift.

Then I turned to Artemis, goddess of the moon, forests, bears, and goals. Artemis is still strong and, possibly, the goddess closest to the wild woman archetype. But she can represent a defense against the vulnerability of loving, whereas my natural way is loving and relating, which are qualities of Aphrodite. The third goddess in this conflict is Hera, a personification of the wife-and-marriage archetype. How to have these three goddesses coexist in one psyche has, of yet, proven difficult because each vies for dominance.

Another significant contribution comes from Jungian analyst Marion Woodman—notably, her 1985 book, *The Pregnant Virgin: A Process of Psychological Transformation*, wherein she examines the process and "ways of restoring the unity of body and soul" (p. 7). That process is important in the alchemy of transformation because once a woman has become more conscious of her wild instincts through the first phase of *unio mentalis*, or knowledge of herself, she later has to unite the whole mind with her body and good instincts—but with consciousness and her moral compass. Woodman describes the struggle to become conscious though the wisdom of the body, initiations, and dreams.

> The heart knows what is real. It beats in the reality of *now*, and when we think with the heart we are not looking back through the misty corridors of the mind. We are in the reality of *now*. . . . Whoever is able to come from that still point is free to be a virgin—free to love and be loved, free to come from an inner center of gravity and free to allow others to come from theirs. (p. 144)

In addition to advocating for awareness of the embodied *now*, Woodman's book also examines the process of becoming conscious of our mother and father complexes, or ghosts of the past. The author further examines how freedom from those hauntings translates into relationships (and so informs that area of this research as well):

> Both partners are attempting to become more conscious of their complexes and their masculine and feminine sides, both are willing to reflect on their interactions, and both have the courage to honor the uniqueness of what they share. Neither is attempting to possess the other, neither wishes to be possessed. (p. 152)

This is a mature, and perhaps idealized, vision for relationship. It is worth striving for by looking at our personal complexes that arise and that are usually triggered within the vessel of the relationship itself. This process, although individual, is activated in a dyad.

Nancy Qualls-Corbett (1988), in *The Sacred Prostitute: Eternal Aspect of the Feminine*, examines and brings to consciousness "aspects of feminine nature which have been misunderstood, devalued or lost to the unconscious; in particular . . . the relatedness of sexuality and spirituality and how each may bring life to the other" (p. 18). Her book moves from a general exploration of women's psychological development into the specific area of sacred sexuality.

In *The Way of All Women*, Harding (1970) writes about most women's instinct to marry. Marriage is an institution she holds in the highest value because "it carries with it the possibility of development on more planes than any other which life offers" (p. 155). That is a bold statement—and an interesting one given that Harding never married, at least in the traditional sense. I have to agree, though, let us use the word *relationship* or *partnership* instead of the word *marriage*. Relationship can pave a path of individuation for those who are impelled by something intense in their own natures to seek for greater heights and depths of emotional experience. Harding differentiates the quality of the Eros function within diverse types of marriages: some "maintain an easy workaday comradeship," whereas some are impelled to "the dark and unknown and violent forces in the depths" (p. 150). The marital pair mirror each other's anima-animus to a certain degree and that an emotionally immature man, for example, will reflect a woman who is immature in her own Eros function of emotional relatedness— a common modern phenomenon because women have further developed their animus function (a woman's inner masculine). Such women are competent and successful business or professional women; they do not need men to be providers. In such cases, the women's psychological task is to develop their feminine values and feeling reactions. Women accessing the wild woman are recovering feminine values and feeling reactions. Many of us have compensated for our grandmothers' dependence on men by becoming competent and successful women; however, the cost may have been our own relationships and feminine values. A woman's relationship with an undeveloped man reflects her own lack of development in relationship. Psychological development requires such women to differentiate the emotional side of their nature. For us, our task is to gain a relation to the feminine principle—the principle of Eros—within ourselves.

Because a woman's relation to the animus is often experienced initially through lived projection, projection and animus are important topics. Marie-Louise von Franz, in her book *Alchemy* (1980a), wrote:

One can only speak of projection when doubt has arisen. . . .
Naturally the onlooker doubts, which is why if one takes a
modern case, for instance X falls in love with Y, the onlooker will call that a projection of the animus. But for the
person involved there is no projection, and it would be an
analytical mistake to say there was—that would be in-
fecting the other person with one's own doubt. For X that
man is now the beloved, and not simply an image of the
animus. If I doubt it because I am not in the same *participation*, I have no right to poison the other with that doubt.
(p. 123)

For the lover, the other is the beloved, not a projection of animus, which
implies that the beloved acts out the role of the archetypal anima or
animus for the lover, and, indeed, it can be *poisonous* to doubt that. At
a certain point, the projection must be removed—though it is not
achieved through willpower or consciousness but through a release
from the archetypal hold on us or, maybe, simply through grace. The
lovers have to relate to each other with consciousness. Von Franz
continued: "Projections die autonomously—suddenly the thing has
disappeared, and that happens completely without conscious coope-
ration. Such things are psychological events *per se*" (p. 123). Hillman
(1972) also wrote of the necessity of relating with another person and
normalizes the feeling of mad impossibility. The struggle with a concrete other person both serves soul and is a path of individuation.
Coming into relationship with the animus archetype is also essential
in this process.

The animus-anima is still, rightly, mysterious. In an earlier paper
titled "Animus and Individuation," I argued that women needed to
develop the animus relationship; but something was not sitting right
with that assertion. With independent women, it is the anima—the
female principle—that requires development. But to confuse the matter
further, I have had dreams in which the animus-anima figure could
shape-shift and change gender. One such dream went like this:

I am hiking in a forest up a mountain; there is a forest fire above, and the firefighters come. I retreat to avoid the commotion. The larger commotion is that the firefighter-guards bring out from the fire what appears to be a woman prisoner. I understand the immensity of her power and give her as much room as possible; just being near her is potentially dangerous. She is beautiful, has a coy grin, and exhibits poise and grace. She shape-shifts into a handsome man, then a large black man in rubber boots, and then back to a beautiful woman again. As a woman, she reveals to me that she is concealing the most lethal of weapons: a mirror and a comb. A firefighter-guard reprimands me for my lack of trust in her. He says, "She walks out of here a free man." I have the sense that she has complete control of all the events playing out.

I awake and think she is both anima-animus and Aphrodite and Artemis all at once—two goddesses who, in my previous under-standing, cannot have a concurrent mode of consciousness. This dream figure is still a mystery. In the context of the wild woman research, this dream preceded my "conscious" work with her by about four months. The only approach for the explorations on the anima-animus is to be a little betwixt and between—and open.

The theory of the anima-animus originated with Jung, who suggested that in a man, the contrasexual image—which usually includes the Eros principle of connecting—is the anima or soul image, whereas the animus is the equivalent in a woman but is about Logos and spirit. Claire Douglas's (2000) *Woman in the Mirror: Analytical Psychology and the Feminine* extensively covers the topic of a woman's animus and the importance of developing that relationship intra-psychically. While hard to define, Douglas cites Harding's definition of the animus and anima.

These figures stem from a very deep source in the unconscious and are only partly available to consciousness.
In addition to being parts of the personality, they partake
of the nature of the archetypes. Jung has called them border
phenomena, standing at the junction of the personal and
collective unconscious. We can only describe them to the
extent that they are manifested in consciousness; we cannot
delimit them completely. (p. 151)

Post-Jungians such as James Hillman have argued that the anima is the
soul image in both men and women. In *A Blue Fire*, Hillman (1989)
wrote about anima consciousness: "Ego tends to regard anima
consciousness as elusive, capricious, vacillating. But these words
describe a consciousness that is mediated to the unknown, conscious
of its unconsciousness and, so, truly reflecting psychic reality" (p. 89).
This is helpful for understanding the mode of anima consciousness,
especially in the context of alchemy. Alchemy and individuation share
the ultimate aim (*telos*) of transformation by uniting the opposites—
ultimately, the *coniunctio* of consciousness with the unconscious. In
Hillman's quote, there is an implication of the necessity of anima
consciousness as the mediator not only to reflect psychic reality but
also to facilitate the ultimate *coniunctio* of conscious with the unconscious.

In a preface to Hillman (1989) Thomas Moore wrote, "Anima and
animus are two very different sources of meaning and fantasy, much
deeper than ego, that are difficult to unite in "marriage" or "syzygy"" p.
36). Hillman's polytheistic approach favors the differentiation of the
anima-animus. Further, he embraces the varied beauty and messy
confusion by saying that "projections occur between parts of the
psyche, not only outside into the world. . . . Each anima figure projects
a particular sort of animus figure and vice versa" (pp. 90-91). Hillman's
work is rich and dense; however, it provides comfort to anyone
immersed in and entangled with the mysterious topic of anima-animus.

Most Jungians seem to agree that the opposite-sex image is inherent in the anima-animus image. There are archetypes that constellate around a contra-sexual image. Jung recognized that the contra-sexual images were so important to the psyche that estrangement from them represented the loss of soul. Most people experience them through projection onto a person of the opposite sex that lends a quality of fascination. The projection creates a numinous field. This work of coming into relationship with the anima-animus is so central to the individuation process that Jung considered it the *magnum opus* of individuation—basically the masterpiece of the work of individuation. This seems fitting for a process that promises to unite the unconscious with the conscious. Another way to imagine it is that the anima and animus unite as the ultimate *hieros gamos* (sacred union) within a personal psyche. Possibly this is where the shape-shifter image begins to present in images.

Because of patriarchal dominance, the animus aspect is likely overdeveloped in *both* men and women, and the work of reclaiming the archetype of the wild woman is closely related to the development of the anima. In other words, a maturation of the feminine soul and its characteristics is required rather than further development of the animus—particularly in women who are so independent that we can provide for and protect ourselves and are not looking to have more children. Some of us are too animus driven and have forfeited an anima-driven capacity. In contrast to Hillman, other post-Jungians, such as Harding and Sylvia Brinton Perera (1981), suggest that some women must learn more receptivity, relatedness, vulnerability, and the ways of women's mysteries in order to achieve more psychological balance. This fits with the overarching evolutionary path offered in this book from the wild virgin to the wild woman. The stronger we get, the more vulnerable we are asked to become—by the experiences life brings us—and the less ego-guarded and defended. We can imagine the animus and the anima are (*at least*) two separate and distinct figures that exist in both men and women, and both require the ego to be in relationship to them. The anima as a guide and an intermediary between worlds would seem to be an expression of the wild woman archetype.

Both Robert Johnson (1989) in *She: Understanding Feminine Psychology* and Erich Neumann (1956) in *Amor and Psyche: The Psychic Development of the Feminine* view the myth of Eros and Psyche as a tale of developing feminine psychology in men and women. That myth is the underlying myth of this book, because it is about joining Love and Soul. This book is an amplification of that myth; however, in those two interpretations, the tale and its tasks are told in a linear way, and the authors have applied chronology to the development of the feminine in a similar way. But the lived experience of the process of developing the feminine consists of circles, spirals, labyrinths, and forests—these are more appropriate images. Nevertheless, working with myth and story in describing an inner process of developing consciousness is helpful. Downing (1990), in her book *Psyche's Sisters: Reimagining the Meaning of Sisterhood*, looked at the Eros and Psyche myth from the perspective of Psyche's envious sisters, who, through their betrayal, pushed Psyche toward her necessary growth. Marie Louise von Franz (2001) in the *Golden Ass of Apuleius: The Liberation of the Feminine in Man* pointed to the biggest shortcoming in considering this myth as symbolic of the development of feminine psychology. She pointed out that the myth was told in the larger context of the masculine hero's journey, and therefore it pertained to the development of the feminine in men, not women. Despite her arguable correctness on that point, this myth still resonates with many women's journeys; as with most myths, it simply transcends gender.

Individuation

As noted, this book takes a flexible perspective on Jung's monotheistic image of the Self as the archetype of wholeness versus a polytheistic view; we have been moving in and out of both fantasies as it serves the exploration. Therefore, some of this section draws upon the Self fantasy, whereas at other times we draw upon Hillman's archetypal psychology and a pantheon of deities. We reference myths, gods, and goddesses from Greek and Roman traditions because they are the origins of the dominant paradigm in the West. Myths are helpful in differentiating and personifying the gods and goddesses, and the symbolic stories can also offer guidance.

Jung wrote about the development of ego as being the task of the first half of life, and Edward Edinger (1972) suggested the shift during the second half of life to an ego-Self axis. There are various ways of imagining that movement and timeframe, but it does seem that a *dark night of the soul*; an illness, accident, love, a child, a divorce, or something unanticipated comes along that catapults us out of the comfort of our lives and into the abyss and uncertainty of the soul. It can be regarded as a spiritual awakening that ushers in an awareness that we are more than our solitary ego. The awareness of this causes transformation that moves us into closer engagement with the Self. The process is cyclical, and we undergo it again and again, in a nearly continuous way throughout our lifetimes. However, some catalysts are much more powerful than others, and they can drop us into utter despair and change us at a fundamental level. It is a process that can take many years with one crisis or *nigredo* experience after another. We do not know, and we do not get to know in advance how long this process may take.

We should learn to trust the process of our own spiritual awakening. It helps if we recognize that there is a process of reorganization of the psyche and personality at work. This process alternates between ego-Self union and then and repeats throughout a lifetime like a cycle or a spiral. In *Ego and Archetype*, Edinger (1972) wrote:

> The process of alternation between ego-Self union and ego-Self separation seems to occur repeatedly throughout the life of the individual both in childhood and in maturity. Indeed, this cyclic (or better, spiral) formula seems to express the basic process of psychological development from birth to death. (p. 5)

It is not entirely important how we imagine this happening—whether cyclical or spiral, monotheistic or polytheistic, but it is important to recognize there is a basic process at work. In the next section, we lean into the Self fantasy, in many ways it is *almost* interchangeable with the wild woman, or psyche, were we to personify it as feminine. I just want to invite whatever images a woman feels comfortable with, including seemingly contradictory ones. According to Edinger and Jung, the Self is the ordering and unifying centre of the total psyche (conscious and unconscious) just as the ego is the centre of the conscious personality. In other words, the ego is the seat of the *subjective* identity, while the Self is the seat of the *objective* identity. "The Self is thus the supreme psychic authority and subordinates the ego to it. The Self is most simply described as the inner empirical deity and is identical with the *imago Dei*." (Edinger, 1972, p. 3). It is important to recognize that Edinger's view is embedded in a monotheistic paradigm, with the Self as the "supreme psychic authority," which is not congruent with the poly-valence of the wild woman, which can include this view *as well as* others. However, his explanation helps us understand that the ego is subordinate to other forces.

The opus of individuation and the alchemy of transformation mean that we become conscious of the unconscious and can consider that we are becoming conscious of the archetypal forces—the gods and goddesses that are acting upon us. The mere fact that we become conscious of an internal pantheon of gods and goddesses does not mean that Aphrodite, Hera, and Artemis, for example, are suddenly going to find some peaceful resolution and an end to strife and conflict. The suffering will remain, but perhaps in becoming conscious of these forces, we can differentiate them from one another and reduce the chances that we will become identified unconsciously with one (or more) of these archetypal forces. The *goal* of individuation is the recognition and *relationship* with the autonomous aspects of the psyche—i.e., coming to terms with that knowledge that we are *not the master of our own house*. That idea—that we are not the master of our own house—is a fabulous image to hold, though if we build creative relationships with the autonomous aspects of the psyche, we can strive to co-create our lives in conjunction with the aspects we are consciously related to. Another helpful image to reflect on is: *we are in psyche* rather than *psyche is in us*.

Back to the caution of our cultural addiction to the so-called development of consciousness. There is an appropriate tension that must be held in that we do not want to pursue consciousness that requires the sacrifice of love, embodiment, being, and, ultimately, living our life just as it is. Through the lens of the wild woman, individuation is not about the pursuit of consciousness but instead, the feminine soul's compulsive yearning and desire for what she loves, which is love. It is not either *consciousness* or *love*, but both, that is holding the tension of the opposites and is what makes individuation different from a Christian moralistic pursuit of some image of perfection. Individuation may not be so much about differentiating from, as it is about relating to. Consciousness is often confused with rational thinking, leading to the notion that to be in a state of *participation mystique* is irrational, a sign of weak ego-development. This is not the case. Rather, individuation involves a relationship with the many *non-rational* elements of the psyche and can appear quite *primitive*. Individuation is a journey that brings us into relationship with our own spirits that reside in the matter of the body—it involves becoming conscious of the mystery that inhabits one's vessel. It is important in the earlier dream about the flask that the vessel is unique—one of a kind—hand-smithed in moon goddess silver by an artisan. This proves true for each one of us; we are uniquely crafted and beautiful vessels. Both realizing our own unique beauty and relating to the spirits contained within are the ideas whereby I define individuation. We talk about it as though it is a process that at some point we complete—that we achieve wholeness or totality—but that is the hero's myth that comes through in that fantasy: the journey itself takes the length of a life.

Individuation serves a sacred function in that it honors the calling and yearnings of the soul, which are unique to each person. Perhaps, ultimately, this book is an endeavor to accomplish simultaneously two tasks. The first, to become conscious of the Western patriarchal paradigm within which we are entrenched—in particular, the power drive associated with the patriarchy and how it operates within. The second task is to relate to the wild woman and bring in her feminine consciousness.

Sacred Experience and Suffering

Often, life brings suffering. It can be a suffering that takes us into deeper engagement with the archetypes that are alive and active in us and that can be treated as a spiritual or sacred practice. Throughout a woman's life, the suffering and the sacred can be directly connected to the individuation process and a woman's psychological development, which may make it more endurable. The depth psychology approach of honoring Jung's process of individuation as representing an expression of the religious function of the psyche takes courage. Some of us simply must do it; the price of ignoring our soul's call is far too high. Others seem to be able to avoid the path of individuation and transformation—and, truthfully, I do not blame them. The path of individuation is not for the fainthearted. *Living*—fully and really living—is also not for the fainthearted, for living means feeling the full range of human emotion, coming to accept all of who we are: shadow and all. It means coming to accept others and their so-called imperfections too. It means accepting that, like life, we are perfect in our imperfections, quirks, nuances, sufferings, moods, hurts, and so on; and we have all been dealt some doozies. This acceptance is distinct from apathy; there is a time for outrage and for taking action toward redemption, but let us start with acknowledgment and acceptance.

Love has been a catalyst for numinous experience in the lives of many a wild woman. To that end, Kahlil Gibran (1923) on love resonates.

But if in your fear you would seek only love's peace and love's pleasure, then it is better for you that you cover your nakedness and pass out of love's threshing-floor, into the seasonless world where you shall laugh, but not all of your laughter, and weep, but not all of your tears.

It is nothing less than a naked threshing that is asked of us if we accept the call to individuation through love. (Not everyone would agree with me that we can avoid the call, but we can anesthetize ourselves by clinging to certainty, medications, and intoxicants to put off answering the call.) To heed the wild woman's call means we must endure looking at all of who we are and learn to sit with all of what we feel. We cannot only become receptive to light, love, peace, pleasure, and joy, because that may not be how the sacred shows up for us individually. It seems that the more we relate to the wild woman, the more chaos and paradox we have to become comfortable tolerating; it is the chaos that seems to deepen us into a soulful engagement with the world—at least initially, and later it may get easier.

There are many ways that that urge to the transpersonal realm can show up in our lives. The urge for and movement toward the sacred, toward love is innate to psychological development. Corbett (2012b) said: "We know when we are in the presence of the holy; the ability to perceive it is as essential as thirst and hunger. We have an ability to perceive it" (n.p.). The movement toward and the ability to perceive the numinous other are instinctual in us. One of the ways we can perceive the other is through a so-called symptom that causes suffering. Symptoms such as neurosis or compulsions are expressions of the soul. In the spirit of following the symptom, these manifestations *are* possibly an expression of the wild woman. In this respect, they are *good,* reminding us just how little control we have over her compulsions. *Good* because the more we go into the affliction, the more we will be led into the realm of the wild woman where we can relate with her.

The strength of the psychological approach is to find meaning in suffering. While some religious traditions try to transcend suffering, suffering cannot be removed; it is part of the human condition. Simply accepting that suffering occurs is important. Lionel Corbett suggested that it is possible that an archetypal ordering both caused the suffering and organized the childhood environment that was responsible for the suffering (2012a, n.p.). We can only speculate about that, but it is effective in considering deeper layers at work. From a depth psychological perspective, it is not enough to say that wounded children are products of their environment as that suggestion drops down only into the personal and personal unconscious level; it does not drop into the archetypal level of the psyche.

The answer to the question regarding *why* we suffer is difficult, though it may be a reflection of the personal experience of the archetype. If the woman has a shadow or a dark side of the divine in her unconscious, that is the quality that will come forward, and we are then dealing with the dark side of the archetype. The way we relate to the archetype affects how the archetype shows up. For example, a compulsion around love that causes suffering may be an invitation to relate with the dark side of both one's self and the wild woman. Aspects of our image of the archetypal that remain unconscious are more likely to make themselves known in ways that invoke suffering. An autonomous, unintegrated complex will stir intense emotional affect. Such intense suffering can force the sufferer into consciousness. Making those complexes conscious is essential to the individuation process. Corbett takes it even further by suggesting that, psychologically, this is equivalent to incarnation of the Self. As we become more conscious, because of our pathology, so the transpersonal Self becomes conscious within our psyche, and this process is one of individuation or incarnation within the individual. We can interchange the wild woman with the Self in that the wild woman also becomes conscious to us and through us as we learn to relate to her, though we want to be mindful of the possibility of becoming inflated with this attitude. We had best try to remain humble and engage with her in a reciprocal, co-creative bond—with deference.

According to Jung's fantasy of dualism and unification, the lifelong movement toward totality and wholeness requires the conscious integration of all aspects of the Self—light and dark, good and bad, pure and evil—"and involves nothing less than a crucifixion of the ego, its agonizing suspension between irreconcilable opposites" (Jung, 1929/1969, p. 44). As we initially begin to become conscious, we feel crucified because the ego suffers immensely. "Jung suggests that we cannot avoid suffering, but we can avoid the worst, which is blind suffering. This approach involves offering one's self as a vessel to the consciousness of "God". In this way, the ego's suffering has meaning, which is to make way for the Self's emerging consciousness.

The healing of suffering is the bringing together of what seems irreparably separate or opposite—the transcendent function discussed earlier. There can be a symbol that arises out of the neurosis from the unconscious that can have a healing effect on us. It could come from a dream, a vision, or some other direct contact with the numinosum. A symbol can come from a dream or from nature, but it may or may not be a spontaneous event; often it is more a process of building an ongoing relationship, and the symbol of the bear or the silver flask are two examples. The wild woman's way is more about relatedness, but the *new attitude* of relatedness itself could be the transcendent function. The third thing ultimately becomes a new perspective or attitude toward the problem.

In order to resolve painful neurosis, we have to move towards the symptom and be willing to look at what we may be ignoring. We want to regard the fixation as a call from the soul. Meaning has the potential to liberate us from the suffering. *Insight alone is insufficient; a total change of attitude is necessary.* Neurosis must be understood as the suffering of a soul that has not discovered its meaning—meaning makes a good many things endurable. I am not suggesting that we can avoid suffering and indeed there are conditions such as intense grief or unrelenting pain where we may never find meaning, though in time we may find greater ease. I am referring to neurotic thoughts as a symptom from the soul. Becoming curious about what could be the latent meaning or value in a symptom can help us understand what the soul is trying to communicate. That in turn helps the god or goddess at the core of the complex become conscious to us—or we may become conscious of the image of the Self within. While this can sometimes liberate us from the complex, it does not always mean the complex will let us go just because we are conscious of it.

Women's psychological development is connected to a sacred, symbolic life that is able to reflect upon and find meaningfulness in our afflictions. This may cultivate a more alive relationship to the archetypes in the psyche. One of the strengths of women engaged with the wild woman is that we have a propensity for relatedness and connection. Engaging with the archetypes of the psyche can be a spiritual practice that hopefully, with time, forges nourishing relationships.

Psyche and Eros

For many wild women, the Psyche and Eros myth can be considered a guide in the process of individuation because the suffering in love is a common catalyst for many of us as we enter the transformation process. Further, many women place love and relationship among their highest values. Jung regarded the process of individuation as the opus of a human life, and he described consciousness as the flower. If we are in the hero myth, then consciousness is the flower; but if we are in the myth of Psyche, of soul, then love, not consciousness, is the telos. As multifaceted women, we are perhaps in service to both love and consciousness, or, perhaps because we live in a culture entrenched in the hero myth, we, too, absorb those values, even though it may not be our personal predominant myth. In the tale, Psyche becomes self-conscious, but it is through her pursuit of Eros, of love; her relationship to Aphrodite; and her courage to encounter Persephone of the underworld. Hillman (1976) wrote on the struggle in the Eros and Psyche myth as "a background to the divine torture of erotic neuroses—the pathological phenomena of a soul in need of love, and of love in search of psychic understanding" (p. 102). Relationship is the catalyst for Psyche's individuation process; to put it another way, relationship serves as the vessel for honoring the soul.

In the Eros and Psyche myth, the theme of light and consciousness can be seen as destructive if too much consciousness is brought in too soon. Von Franz (1980b) wrote about that problem.

This motif is most surprising because we are accustomed to think that light in general is only positive. Light is a symbol for consciousness. . . . Here there is a kind of mystical union between two loving partners, which is fed by mystery. . . . But the moment light falls on it there is separation and suffering and perhaps even the definite destruction of the possibility of redemption. . . . It is an archetypal motif, which means that it is most widespread and important. Consciousness is destructive and causes separation within a certain realm, which is clearly charac- terized as the realm of Eros. It is here that the light of consciousness can have a completely destructive effect. *One has the feeling also, from the way the light disappears, that if the girl could have held on to the mystery and gone on with it indefinitely, then some redemption would at some time have taken place* [emphasis added].

Naturally, the intrusion of the light has to do with the fact that it was brought in too soon. (p. 111)

There is something in this issue of consciousness and love that seems critical and actually antithetical to those of us who cannot help but pursue self-knowledge—it is that in pursuing self-knowledge, by bringing consciousness into the realm of Eros, we may betray our own love. Psyche brings in consciousness too early with the lamp; perhaps the myth reminds us that this unavoidable. The tale tells us the way through once that has happened, as though the poison of her suspicion may be an inevitable part of the process to begin Psyche's journey to mature love. However, like von Franz, I wonder whether it is avoidable, if we can endure holding the tension and not bring too much light to the realm of love too soon and actually allow it to be a long, slow road. We do not know whether von Franz is right, that if Psyche could have held on to the mystery and gone on with it indefinitely, then some redemption would at some time have taken place. Maybe that notion is yet another ploy by the ego to try to avoid suffering.

This idea of *modifying* the myth is similar to Jung's (1958/2010) suggestion in *Answer to Job* that "god" becomes conscious through us and that as *we* evolve, the gods, goddesses, and archetypes transform as well. It is a slow process outside our will that the archetypes transform through our relationships to them. The Eros and Psyche myth is organically evolving after nearly 2,000 years (having originated in the late second century CE). That larger shift is important as we witness and participate in the emergence of the humanization of psyche, of the wild woman. Where we experience more rapid change is not in the archetype per se but in our *relationship* to her; it is the *relationship* that changes, not so much the archetype—at least at the personal level. Myths remain relatively fixed as models of particular ways of being in the world. There is a caution: imagining that we can change an aspect— say, the unconscious masculine that lives in us into a more evolved conscious masculine—actually gives more power to the unconscious because now we have denied it. Of course, anything that falls into unconsciousness has autonomy and is therefore at its most potent in how it affects us.

Perhaps without her sisters to plant the seeds of doubt about her beloved's true identity, Psyche would have just remained in the dark, unconscious and unaware of her own Selfhood. In *Psyche's Sisters: Reimagining the Meaning of Sisterhood*, Downing (1990) wrote:

> Psyche's sisters are envious and cruel—but they push her in the way her soul requires (whereas Eros would happily have kept her in the dark). I have come to see Psyche's sisters as initiating us into an appreciation of how our sisterly relationships challenge and nurture us, even as we sometimes disappoint and betray one another. (p. 4)

From a somewhat optimistic view, we are in a win-win situation. If we can hold the tension and not bring too much analytic consciousness into a romantic relationship, we will be brought closer to love, or, if we cannot, we will follow the journey of Psyche and still be brought closer to love. Maybe this is ultimately the psyche's ever-corrective drive toward love and perhaps also toward wholeness or totality, as in Jung's description. Maybe this is the soul's way of being ever-changing and ever-responding.

Where is Eros in the myth? He is in his mother's complex—his mother complex—in his mother, Aphrodite's, tower—there to do her bidding as a son-lover and not yet a sovereign being. Somehow the feminine soul's coming into relationship with the goddess of love calls forth the mature masculine in Eros at the end of Psyche's fourth task, when she returns from the underworld with Persephone's cask of beauty ointment. Neumann (1956) wrote: "Through the perfection of her femininity and love she calls forth the perfect manhood of Eros. In abandoning herself out of love, she unwittingly achieves redemption through love" (pp. 125-126). This is a seductive sentiment; it appeals to the conscious ego aspect and perhaps to an old belief system. The sentiment, although seductive, dangerously and incorrectly conflates *soul* with *woman*, and *beloved* with *man*. Further, there is a terrible risk of staying in this idea that flawless perfection is somehow achievable in our mortal state; that idea further perpetuates wounding to the psyche.

The hero myth is hard to escape and often moves into dominance, probably out of cultural conditioning. Neumann slipped into it; indeed, *I* also slip into it. Nevertheless, opening the cask of beauty ointment and falling into unconsciousness is what reunites Psyche with her beloved. We can consider that the naive young soul transforms from narcissistic beauty to the beauty of love because she has traversed into her depths and knows herself: her strengths, weaknesses, feelings, and values. That action of opening the cask is the soul surrendering to love, connection, and beauty as her highest ideals rather than self-conscious-ness. Those are Aphrodite's values, too, and in this way, Psyche is perhaps a mortal version or, possibly, a prefiguration of the great goddess. Though she goes unconscious, it is not regressive but, rather, as a rebirth as she awakes anew.

A Human Ending as a New Beginning

My critique of the Eros and Psyche myth is that Psyche cannot retain her humanness at the end; she becomes divine and joins Eros and the rest of the pantheon on Olympus. From one perspective, we can say she realized the Self within, her own god-nature; but I do not care for that interpretation; it falls flat. She begins her journey as a human; her conclusion would have been successful if she could embrace her mortality. By her joining the gods, it is as though the feminine soul had regressed to the archetypal level of the collective unconscious, and culturally, that is what has happened to the human soul. Von Franz (1980b) shares that same concern.

> The marriage takes place not on earth but on Olympus, Psyche is carried off to the realm of the gods, and Eros does not come down to earth. This means that both figures vanish into the collective unconscious. The motif of the holy marriage, the union of the opposites, sinks once again into the unconscious. (p. 129)

A modern-day rewriting of that myth would perhaps have Psyche remain in her human form as we witness the emergence of the wild woman in individuals and in the collective. Psyche does not belong in the realm of the gods; she belongs embodied in matter—in men and women.

While we cannot rewrite myth, we can fantasize about how this story could end differently. Maybe Eros falls in love with a mortal woman who retains her human vulnerability, which *is* what makes her beautiful. The ultimate *coniunctio* then would be possible between spirit (Eros as a god) and matter (Psyche as a mortal). Love remains an archetypal experience, but soul does not transcend her incarnation. This would cause the psychological movement in the West to change from upward—and escaping from life—to downward, incarnating into the body, the being, and into life. What we are witnessing at this time is the wild woman, living out the archetype through embodiment. We are vessels who are receiving input from the wild woman as she emerges, and perhaps Psyche no longer needs her wings to carry her away from incarnation and mortality.

For those of us engaging with the wild woman, it is best to simultaneously reflect on the development of the masculine aspect within us. The anima-animus is a tricky, slippery concept that does not want to be pinned down too completely. As a mediator between the conscious and the unconscious, we cannot fully grasp it, and that is as it should be. In this section, we work with the animus as the masculine spirit image. Women need to develop relationships to both masculine and feminine aspects in order to move toward greater love, beauty, and appreciation of life.

My first conscious meeting of the animus came in a dream three years prior to writing this: *He was barely conscious and barely breathing. I said, "We have to get him on his feet. He's not a vacuum."* I began walking and hiking daily after that dream, and this man was present with me imaginally. The real-world man I was newly falling in love with was my tenant in a suite of my house, the bear-man. Part of the challenge was that I was somewhat conscious that I would be projecting my animus onto him and because of that, I could not just let it flow naturally; I analyzed. I projected onto him an instinctual, sexual, wild man, challenging the patriarchal model, because I saw him as spending much of his time in the mountains as a passionate, Olympic snowboarder—a puer. Instinctual, sexual, wild, vocationally passionate, athletic, and challenging the dominant paradigms: all of them qualities I recognized I needed to develop and integrate. I recognized him as a bear-man—not the kind of man who would behave predictably and merge, bond, or mate, as I wanted to with him. This frustrated, insatiate desire for committed and monogamous relationship was the source of my struggle and neurotic suffering as I came up against myself in the forms of my values, desires, fears, insecurities, jealousy, possessiveness, anxieties, tolerances, and so on; and I had to repeatedly keep going deeper and deeper into them. That was where I found the meaning that enabled me to endure the suffering of the transformative process. Or as my therapist said, I made lemonade out of lemons.

Then there were the bear dreams—hundreds of them—and real bears in my outer world that appeared sometimes daily for a period in the summer. I often encountered dream bears and real bears—nervously at first—and then, eventually, I came to love bears. I initially recognized the bear as a symbol for my growing relationship to both the animus and the bear-man. I refer to this man as my *partner*—not in the mated sense (because it is important to say that he was not my lover by *his* choice) but in the alchemical sense whereby he and I had some sort of soul bond that was mutually contributing to our separate psychological transformations. We struggled anytime we tried to bring lamplight, clarity, or definition to the nature of our relationship: "We are like two magnets that for some reason need each other," he said one day while fidgeting with some magnetized hematite of mine. I later gave him those two pieces of hematite, and he told me he keeps them at his bedside. Perhaps that says more than our words can. We eventually learned to relate without being overly analytical, and with time, the suffering and the struggle released. The gift from it—which is to say, how it became meaningful—was that I discovered myself outside of culture: my personal ideals, values, and feelings.

Animus projection is a tricky term, because *projection* is usually defined as necessarily unconscious, that is, unperceived and un-intentional, a transfer of subjective psychic elements onto an outer object. We see in someone something that is not there, or, if there, only to a small degree. Though, seldom, if ever, is nothing of what is projected present in the object. Many of us—particularly if we are introspective—are usually somewhat conscious and are also perceptive, and what we are projecting may actually be there in the other person; indeed, there is probably always a hook. The seeing of qualities in another—in particular, another that enlivens something in us—is a way of personifying and can show us the qualities we must come into relationship with. For example, we project onto or perceive in a man certain qualities that attract us, and then we recognize them as qualities we must come into relationship with in ourselves in order to develop our animus relationship. Of course, that raises the problem of analyzing the relationship and bringing too much light into the realm of Eros. Further, it attempts to define something mysterious. Additional realizations may continue to come years after the initial relationship that kindles the process; later, I saw other qualities in this man that were needing to come out of my shadow. There were qualities in him that came to my awareness, and I am sure that more will follow. The men we fall for, who bear our projection, often behave in a manner that pushes us to grow and change our perspectives and attitudes because those men refuse to conform to our old ways. In this way, the animus can be a guide to both the inner and outer worlds.

We need not consider an attraction to be rooted in a projection if there is no discordance between what we imagine and the reality that is presented. However, it can be hard to know whether what we imagine and the reality present are in accord because it is impossible to know others' experiences of their realities; indeed, it is hard enough to know our own realities, which are so polyvalent and multidimensional that it is like looking through a kaleidoscope. Words like *reality* and *truth* imply that there are only *one* reality and *one* truth, but in fact there are multiple realities and multiple truths depending on which archetypal lens we are looking through. Such thinking serves to add to the complexity and deepen such concepts, and although confusing, it is the wild woman's way.

We can be aware of our own animus projection to some degree— and of projective identification as anima women as well; however, awareness alone is not enough to make the struggle any easier. In theory, when we recognize our projection, we can try to remove it from the person and allow the myth to live out imaginally in our fantasy world—without acting on it externally. Woodman (1990) wrote:

> Masculinity and femininity [are] two energies within each
> individual, both striving toward an inner harmony. So long

as these energies are projected onto others, we rob ourselves of our own maturity and our own freedom. Until we
take responsibility for these projections, genuine relationship is impossible because we are entangled in our own
images instead of relating to new possibilities that expand
our boundaries. (p. 9)

We can certainly strive for such harmony, but we also do well to
surrender and accept where we are; it is maybe not even possible to will
ourselves to disentangle from our images, so we can just try to be
conscious of the soul's longing for love and just be with that *normal*
pathological tendency. However, to reframe Woodman's quote from the
wild woman's perspective, entanglement in the images is what causes
new possibilities that expand our boundaries. Genuine relationship
does include such entanglements; without them, we remain static and
harden and do not transform.

Many a woman knows of the longing and yearning for the man
who carries her animus projection, but the longing is also for
relationship to spirit; the animus is close to the archetypal and, as such,
is a bridge to the divine. The longing never goes away for very long,
and when it does, sometimes there is peace, and other times there is
longing for longing. The soul simply desires authentic closeness.
Acceptance of the yearning as a signal to something more soulful and
meaningful makes it somewhat more bearable. There are times when I
am writing, practicing yoga, hiking, eating and sleeping well, present
with my son, or sharing in intimate company that my yearning
diminishes or, sometimes, falls away, and I feel peaceful—free. Sometimes though, the absence of the yearning can feel like a void or
inertness and we can wonder: What next? The yearning is useful in
guiding us toward a purposeful, meaningful life.

Removing projections is a messy and difficult task. It is not a
matter of knowing of the reality of the anima and animus that causes
the projection to no longer occur. This is an impossible goal. It is
through becoming aware of the projection that it becomes possible for

us to see in reflection the contents of our own psyches that otherwise might escape us. Projection is an important part of falling in love, which is often what draws two people together in the first place so that human-to-human relatedness can evolve and occur at some point. That connectivity and attraction facilitate both the inner relationship to the anima-animus and the eventual human relatedness. Relationship with a member of the opposite sex creates the conditions for us to work on the anima and animus problem, and, conversely, a good rapport with our anima and animus is of great value in working out our human relationships. Projection is unavoidable and a natural occurrence; it is neither good nor bad. It is somewhat helpful to recognize yearning for another as the longing for the *coniunctio* with one's own deep soul, in part—and, in part, it is simply at face value: the human yearning for authentic, human, intimate relationship.

Initially, the animus is unconscious in most, if not all, women until we become mature and self-aware enough to be able to develop the animus relationship. Once the animus relationship is made conscious and differentiated, then the animus can ideally serve as a guide for the woman. There are nearly as many views and theories on the anima-animus as there are theorists; however, in keeping with several post-Jungians—including Wheelwright, Harding, and Bins-wanger—the optimal role of the positive animus can be as a creative tool and provide the stamina for her endeavors. The positive animus can be a bridge to the archetypes that guide our inner lives.

We can trace the development of the animus through women's dreams. Initially, the dream males may develop from violent oppressors and cruel judges to friendlier, more helpful figures, then to equal or supporting figures that stand beside the dreamer or even behind her, and finally the androgyne. Some theorists insist that this is a linear progression, and no stage can be missed. My experience is that it is more like smoke curling upward. Occasionally, the tyrannical father will still come, even though there are also several visits by androgynous, trickster, shape-shifter, and shaman figures. As we change paradigms from egocentrism to recognizing and relating to the plurality of archetypes that reside within, it can feel like one step forward and two steps back. I do not experience the process as linear, but there are distinct changes in who is in my dreams and how I relate to them.

Woodman (1990) tells a personal story that demonstrates her relationship with her animus. She was not able to speak publicly to share her ideas with the world: "My inner Luke had disappeared and with him went my creative imagination, that spirit that brings 'light to the sun and music to the wind.' While I was conscious enough to know that life could not be Paradise, I also knew it was never meant to be an endless load of duty and responsibility" (p. 108). She was speaking of her animus that had left the service of her soul work and been seduced away by false standards. Optimally, the animus serves as a guide for a woman. Once my therapist gently nudged: did I ever think my bear-man was a guide for my inner life? "No." And I was in my second year of depth psychology. In retrospect, of course, I realize that was precisely what he was.

When the positive animus is used intrapsychically, rather than projected, it becomes an instinctive awareness that guides her toward becoming more authentically herself. As a powerful instinctive force and aspect of my animus figure, the bear—transformed into a guide who knows what to do—speaks to my personal experience. As we let go of our need to have our plans mapped out and life figured out, we become more confident in our ability to figure it out as we go. There are ease and trust in this place—even amidst the ever-increasing tension and uncertainty—though I will complicate this by suggesting that the bear-animus instinctive guidance is also a derivative of the wild woman. The animus is positioned in the psyche between the collective and objective psyche. In this way, it is often thought to be a psychopomp that can traverse the deep realm of the unconscious or the imaginal world and is connected with soul, creativity, and sexuality. Most of us rarely use this intrapsychically, we fall in love and then are possessed by that very projection. I fell in love with my partner, but I was thwarted from being able to merge or lose myself, and I kept being forced into self-reflection; therefore, the external served as a catalyst for the development of my animus relationship.

The senex, as patriarch, has been dominating the culture and inner lives of men and women; here we explore the relationship of senex, puer, and animus. The opposite of the senex shows up as the puer, or eternal boy, and the men that my animus projection falls on are men strongly in this puer archetype: they rebel against an overly one-sided patriarchal view and bring in new energy. In my psyche, the puer and the animus are closely linked, and I have had to work on becoming conscious of the senex and patriarchal domination to breathe in new spirit and provide a different perspective from the dominant old one. Hillman (2005) in *Senex and Puer* wrote about the senex-puer syzygy as a constellated archetypal pairing. We want to strive to create conditions wherein they can work harmoniously together.

I had a dream that seemingly contradicted my conscious belief of my partner's being predominantly a puer type.

> *I am sexual with my partner, but he keeps changing into my ex-husband. I can't tell them apart, they are so closely identical. Yes, it is my beloved, but he is so much like my ex-husband, it is very confusing and surprising.*

This was the night after I had a taxing encounter with my ex-husband, whom I experience as a man with a predominant senex aspect. Why would he show up as nearly indivisible from my partner, whom I consciously perceive as culturally defiant? Initially, this dream forced me to look deeply at my partner and his relationship to the patriarchal dominant—in particular, to recognize his relationship to his feelings, his drive to compete and dominate in his sport, and his quest for self-perfection. Then I explored the next layer: where in me are these patriarchal values still playing out? On even further reflection, I considered the constellation of the senex-puer syzygy that Hillman describes. Perhaps this pairing is unifying and starting to relate through me in a more cooperative way as the positive senex gives the discipline and structure needed to realize the puer's (my animus's) ideas and actions.

Another dream supports this line of inquiry:

> *I am at a restaurant, and an older man at my table invites the youth—who are segregated in another room—to join us. The older woman restaurateur approves, and they, with their round table, join us, with our square table, in the great room.*

I have never had what I would consider a positive relationship to the dominant patriarchy, but these dreams are heartening that this relationship is transforming; as well, the square and the round as alchemical symbols are also united. I thought of the Knights of the Round Table with the youth bringing in their table to share with ours. Also, my conscious attitude is still at the table with the senex, though he is a bit of a rebel himself, because it was uncouth that he would invite the youth to join us, and we thought the matriarch—the *big* boss—might be disgruntled; but instead, she gave a knowing smile and nod and prepared the drinks for the youth who had joined us.

In keeping with the slippery nature of defining the anima and animus, we have to honor and hold open space for the possibility that it is actually one archetype that personifies as male or female. During this research, I had a number of dreams of the anima-animus as a shape-shifter. In particular, the previously mentioned dream in which the woman-man changed shape as she walked out of the burning forest "a free man," with her comb and mirror. This anima-animus figure was potent. She reminded me of both Aphrodite with her beauty accoutrements and Artemis in her virgin wood, which was set ablaze as she passed. Her mirror of reflection could be turned inward or outward, and such reflection had the power to destroy life as the ego knew it. The wild woman figure was revealing herself in her multifacetedness and ambiguous nature. In this dream, the wild woman was being liberated.

I had another significant dream that speaks to the out-of-the-box, out-of-the-collective framework and that also addresses the anima-animus as shape-shifter.

I am in a box about the size of an elevator; a fat mama brown bear and her three cubs saunter in, pleased to find me. I know they have been looking for me, and I have no fear except a sense of concern for the well-being of the cubs because I know they would not thrive in a box; they are in danger. I lead all of them out of the box in search of a natural habitat for them. There is a path that branches off, but a polar bear is there, and I know it would be a threat to the bear cubs, so that is clearly not the way, either. Then the mama bear stands up and turns into a tall, lean man. I am with a friend, and I say, "Did you see that?" She-he-bear says, "Of course, bears are shape-shifters. What did you expect?" I knew that, but I needed confirmation; and I realize my friend is also a man-woman-bear and, in fact, I may be as well. I just accept that it is confusing to know who is what, but I have got to get these cubs to safety, and that's all that matters. Now the mama-bear-man is an erotic companion, and he has entrusted the cubs to me and will meet up with me soon. I get the cubs to the edge of a cedar forest, and we wait there for him. We are where we need to be for now.

There was a sense of being guided by those very curious beings to get out of the box (the dominant paradigm). I think the cubs represented creative projects in the young stages that all seem to belong outside the collective space and in a wilder, more natural environment. I feel guided by my dream friend. The mama-bear-man, as an incarnation of the wild woman, and even the coldness of the polar bear that is showing me which way not to go. I note that I am *not* afraid of bears any longer, and I also accept the topsy-turvy world of the shape-shifter. That speaks to developing the relationship with the wild woman. In this way, these archetypes can now guide me on my path to a natural, soulful environment as represented by the forest, which is perhaps also the wild woman in still another guise. Each woman will have her own dreams and guides on her journey; some of these figures are universal in nature, so they may appear to others; and bears certainly seem to grace the terrain of many women's inner forests. We want to welcome these guests as they come to us as guides and ask us to develop relationships with them.

Feminine

In addition to the evolving relationship with the masculine, a woman is best served if she simultaneously comes into relationship with the wild woman. The wild woman certainly does not want to be caught—butterfly that she is. Nevertheless, we have to try to clarify the use of these terms. I suggest that the anima is the feminine soul image in both men and women. In women, that is an aspect of the wild woman and can sometimes be interchangeable as a personification of a woman's soul, but the wild woman is closer to the instinctual body. Like the anima-animus, the wild woman is a mediator between conscious and unconscious realms, though she is also known through women's embodiment. In the tale, if Psyche remained human, this is who the wild woman would be. The wild woman is the embodied, vulnerably human personification of a woman's essence, her soul.

The night before I began this section on the feminine in women's psychological development, I had a short but potent dream.

> I suddenly have a boy child; he is mine, but it's not clear whether I gave birth to him or, more specifically, when that happened, but he is my child. Then I understand: he is the offspring of the moon goddess, and she is the one who impregnated me. I feel I have been given the most valuable treasure, beyond what I could even imagine; I am flooded with love and gratitude.

I have had many dreams about children over the years, especially since I had my son who is now eight years old. However, this dream had a different magic to it, because, of course, I was vessel and guardian of a child of the moon goddess. Psyche is so interesting in her words. Why the *moon goddess*? Why not the *wild woman*? I associated and amplified *moon goddess*: I have a silver tattoo of a feminine moon spirit on my calf. I always refer to menstruation as *moontime*—the reproductive cycle of a woman's body intertwined with the lunar cycle, which for me is usually a time of building tension, then quiet reflection, and, often, new revelations. Notably, this dream happened on the night of the Taurus full moon—a moon that invites us to open our senses to the sensual and celebrate the beauty of each moment. I initially considered Artemis as the moon goddess. Then I was pointed toward Selene as a much earlier Titan goddess of the moon who represents the moon personified as a divine being. Selene's beloved was the puer prince Endymion, with whom she is said to have had 50 children.

We want to be careful with this child offered by the moon goddess and not try to label it. Nevertheless, I felt urged to look up *Divine Child* in Woodman's (1985) *The Pregnant Virgin: A Process of Psychological Transformation*, a book I had read about five years earlier. "One child, however, is noticeably different from the others. It has Presence. It is a Divine Child . . . with its birth, the old gods have to go" (p. 23). This resonated. The child is, in part, also the gift of this book itself, because without the moon goddess's imbuing of my life, my work, my psyche, my whole being, there would be no creative work—no divine child. I thought he may also be a new animus figure in my life and a new conscious attitude that has gestated and emerged out of the feminine.

Although many of us physically transition from maiden to mother when we have our children, we do not always make the transition psychologically—though that time can be the beginning of the transformation process. It is poignant that one of the significant amplifications of the bear is as the mama bear, that fierce protector of her young. This proved to be a harder aspect of this archetype for me to become conscious of and to integrate. It can be hard for many of us to fully become mothers. There is also the significant aspect in the dream that this new life is both seeded and gestated by the feminine; the masculine is not involved in this creation. This boy child is the offspring of the feminine only. What would a masculinity created solely of the feminine be like? We can consider the Christian story of Christ born from the virgin feminine. This story is similar with Mary being impregnated by the Holy Spirit. The Holy Spirit is not explicitly male, though Christ as the Son of God implies the divine masculine is responsible for the child's birth. I have not reached the depth of the mystery of the meaning of the moon goddess's having impregnated me with a divine child. I just have a felt sense that it is both an honor and a significant responsibility. I hope I can serve her well by caring for the boy.

During the same night, I suffered dreams of a father figure who was trying to seduce me in order to appropriate my power. Considered on a symbolic level, I see this as the old god of patriarchy personified as my father still working to subvert this new attitude and feminine force in me, this gift of this child that the moon goddess had entrusted to my care. A further amplification of this dream harkens to the fairy tale of Rumpelstiltskin. In the end of the tale, Rumpelstiltskin wants nothing less than the miller's daughter's most soulful possession, her child. In the dream, while I was endeavoring to be gracious to him in order not to alert him to my intention to escape, I was also looking for a new place to live and renovating an existing structure. He wanted what I had, which was new blood and breath for his old outmoded ways, but there was no way he would be able to succeed. His presence was that of the "lecherous old man" (von Franz, 1999, p. 69). In *The Cat: A Tale of Feminine Redemption*, von Franz (1999) writes:

> The old conscious attitude now wants to have that newly redeemed feminine for himself . . . to integrate or to profit from the renewal of life that has come forth in another domain. He wants to assimilate it and would kill it if he could. (p. 118)

Von Franz goes on to tell about a conversation between her and Jung, in which Jung said:

> The past is like an enormous sucking wind that sucks one back all the time. If you don't go forward you regress. You have to constantly carry the torch of the new light forward. . . . So the overcoming of the old emperor [father] means to be absolutely inexorable, ruthless about what is different and new. (p. 120)

What is different and new is the wild woman, as well as the child the moon goddess has gifted. The mother bear is protective of this child, and such is perhaps the energy required to keep moving forward and not get sucked back into the past; to prevent the old fathers from appropriating the new life to refill their outmoded ways. Ferociousness is required to protect the new child—our creative ideas, aspirations, and values—and stand up against the old attitude. There are certain endeavors that one must speak up for, and fight for, because otherwise the vital energy is lost. We must resist the old, intrapsychic patriarch.

A woman in a psychological transformation process at mid-life can be thought of as a pregnant virgin, which is similar to the metaphor of the caterpillar, chrysalis, and butterfly. In ancient Greece, the soul was often imagined as a butterfly, and the word for soul was *psyche*, just like in the tale. The pregnant virgin experiences a psychological pregnancy in which the woman gives birth to her own soul. Once we are conscious of our soul, we are imbued with her creativity. A woman becoming conscious of her soul may have dreams of discovering a little girl, but probably one who has been neglected or perhaps hiding under the stairs for many years. This new consciousness suddenly appears once the old mother and father are out of the way. Once we have found this little girl, we bring her to maturity and health and watch her grow through our dreams.

> Eventually she becomes a conscious virgin who, when she's
> strong enough, is penetrated by the masculine. It's always
> a mystery who the lover is—she is suddenly pregnant . . .
> then that girl will bring forth a glorious boy—a golden boy,
> a child with wonderful energy. (Woodman, 1985, p. 61)

Woodman's "pregnant virgin" and "golden boy" resonate with my dream of the moon goddess; however, my dream is significantly different in that the feminine is *not* "penetrated by the masculine." Women engaging with her are given the creative seed by the feminine alone. This is not to fall back to some overly defended place of "I do not need a man." It is to say, however, that some mysteries belong wholly to the feminine. It is possible that Woodman's pregnant virgin who has been penetrated by the masculine is more a model for individuation in the traditional paradigm, but that the theme of women's becoming impregnated by the moon goddess is emergent culturally and, simultaneously, is older than time.

A new worldview creates fear and conflict for the ego that is identified with the patriarchal power system—the only paradigm it has ever known. Out of an effort to self-protect, the ego resists; therefore, patience and kindness are required as we tend to the images from our dreams and the affects in our bodies. A metaphor comes to mind: if we take antibiotics too often—or expand consciousness too rapidly—we become immune, and the ego adapts and finds trickier places to hide and then embeds the patriarchal dominant even deeper. An ego unconsciously identified with the patriarchal dominant does not readily give up its power in place of love. In order to subvert the dominant authority, the wild woman does best to proceed wisely, not calling attention to herself by carrying too much light in the wrong environment.

As women become more autonomous from the dominant cultural values and perspectives through much self-reflection, we foster a healthy new masculine aspect, a positive animus. Woodman (1993) wrote about a new masculine born from the pregnant virgin.

I think there's a masculinity we have little knowledge of. We've done a lot of work on the feminine, but just as exciting is the masculinity born of that virgin feminine. A woman first has to work through her needs, her feelings and her values. Then the masculine grows up and says, "I will stand up for them; I will put them out there in the world and I will work with you in all your creative activity." (p. 61)

This is the inner masculine voice we want to nurture and cultivate. Here we have the term *virgin* again, but we can consider it more deeply in a new way in this context. No longer in the way of the self-possessed, "I don't need a man." Yes, she is still a woman who is one in herself—who belongs to herself—a woman who is free of the old complexes. The complexes remain, but she relates to them from a mature ego standpoint. The wild woman is virginal insofar as she, too, is one in herself, but that does not diminish her need or valuing of transformative relationship and love. In fact, it may accentuate it. This new masculinity is interested in genuine empowerment grounded in instincts and supports the woman. It is not in the hero myth of slaying the dragon or the great serpent—images close to the symbol of the feminine—in favor of soul-making through metaphor and creative acts. This is a new masculinity that operates from love and not power. So many of us agree about the importance of Jung's sentiment that *the opposite of love is not hate but power*. This way of relating between the new feminine energy and the new masculine energy in individual and collective psyches is a harbinger of hope and love. Woodman (1985) ends *Addiction to Perfection* on a promising note.

If [a woman] abdicates her throne, then . . . she joins the race of "mere humanity." With arms wide open she welcomes Life and Love. . . . She is a human being, and being human she is able to give and to receive the greatest of all human gifts—"I love you as you are." (pp. 189-190)

What does "*abdicates her throne*" mean? I understand it as giving up ego control and becoming a feminine receptacle of love. There is also a challenge to a woman's sovereignty with that image, to become part of the greater community and interconnectedness. The wild woman's consciousness allows for life to flow, as she remains embodied, open, flexible, and responsiveness.

It is important to briefly differentiate the inviolate virgin—such as Athena, Artemis, or Aphrodite—from the Kore that is represented in the innocence of Persephone as the naive maiden under the protection of her mother, Demeter. The rape of the virginal Kore is an archetypal experience that deepens a woman's downward and inward movement and "is not only possible, but is absolutely necessary" (Berry, 2001, p. 203). The inviolate virginity of Artemis or Aphrodite, for example, cannot be raped without decimating the archetype; these two types of virginities (Kore and inviolable) are entirely different archetypal experiences. Further, each of the virgin goddesses also represents very different forms and experiences of virginity.

Culturally, we can become defended when we speak of rape, because it is a literal horror; so, regarding the rape of Persephone as maiden, we are speaking of an intrapsychic maturation process whereby the innocent and narcissistic young feminine must have the ground fall out from under her so she can learn of her own depths. In "Climbing the Alchemical Mountain," Perluss (2008) explored this.

> That which at first feels like an attack from the outside is later discovered within oneself. In other words, Persephone is taken by her own instinct. Essentially, she rapes herself. She tears apart her own innocence because deep down she knows that the sacrifice of innocence—that unconscious state of passivity—is a fundamental aspect of being a complete woman. (p. 95)

The violation of such naive innocence is part of the process that gives rise to the new virginal feminine—the inviolable feminine—as a woman who knows her own needs, feelings, and values. This is not an inviolable woman who remains unaffected by love and becomes hardened and rigid; it is a woman who is open to being changed by love, who knows the sacredness of her body as a vessel for spirit, and who values the one precious life she has.

Open to Life

There are many ways to reject life beyond rejecting food and succumbing to other addictions. There is also staying in degenerative relationships or jobs or simply following our modern way of uninterrupted activity, go-go-go, and never allowing the slower receptivity of the feminine nature to be honored—not being with our own Being. It is much harder and more terrifying to really live a life. It is incredibly risky, and suffering is unavoidable if we choose to "hide in the middle of the flames" (Woodman, 1993, p. 8). Unconsciously, I had probably been highly ambivalent about living; maybe that was why I feared the ambivalence of the gods, goddesses, and archetypes.

I would often be psychologically absent. Maybe I was distracting myself with busyness or getting tuned out on a computer, or denying my embodied experience by engaging in spiritual ascetic practices when in fact my preference was to be with the spirit world rather than the human. A few more years into the metamorphosis, and I ached to really live far out on the high limb and deep down into the roots. Then a few more years again into the metamorphosis, and I just wanted a simple life—less digging around in the psyche and more just living my life: walking my son to school, cooking meals, having good conversation, making a campfire. When I reach the end of my life, I want to feel that I loved, laughed, and cried with all that I had. It is not that I want to *do* more; in fact, I prefer to do less. It is that I want to be more fully engaged in my living. This choice to live is a necessary step in connecting with the wild woman who wants to live embodied through us. David Whyte (1990) wrote about opening to life in his poem "Enough."

Enough. These few words are enough.
If not these words, this breath.
If not this breath, this sitting here.

This opening to the life
we have refused
again and again
until now.
Until now.

I love this poem. I read it at Christmas dinner, where it was well received; we all felt just being together was enough.

Von Franz wrote about how after many years of analysis, her colleagues bring in such complicated dreams, as though the unconscious were trying to wean the analysand from wanting to make use of its advice. The dreams then have "much more to do not with insight but with simply being, teaching people to be, teaching people not to have insight or to realize things, but teaching them just how to be" (p. 107). She goes on to tell a story from Zen Buddhism about an old man with a beggar bowl after great enlightenment: "He has forgotten the gods, he has forgotten the enlightenment, he has forgotten everything, but wherever he walks, the cherry tree blossoms" (Spiegelman & Miyuki, 1985, p. 113). Von Franz (1990) explained it.

> Naturally this forgetting is not a regression. It is not simply a return to the previous unconsciousness. It's still progress. It's a progression to Taoist uselessness, to just being. And the whole intellectual aspect of the analysis, that one always searches for insight and for instruction from the unconscious, to a great extent goes away. That would be the higher aim. (p. 107)

It is such a humorous paradox that we struggle and strive to make meaning, to understand, to receive guidance, to wake up!—to finally *just be*. The aim, if there is an aim, is to eventually simply live our lives after the hard-won reward of waking up.

There is so much wit and wisdom in simplicity, yet it is necessary to go through the pain of awakening. Otherwise, one remains zombie-like, the walking dead, never really living one's own life—never really free of the lecherous old patriarch and lethargic old matriarch. It can be too easy, and too common, for a woman to say, "I'm just living my life," as an excuse to not "wake up," but in fact she is not living her life; she is still living her life unconsciously. Ultimately, we strive to find a new way of being in the world, and then, eventually, we just live it. To apply alchemy to this stage, this is the completion of the second stage where the soul rejoins the body; the *unio mentalis* and the body unite but with consciousness intact and not in the form of a regression to the previous, unconscious condition. The psyche has been reorganized around the Self and the ego is of service to the Self. It is possible that the full completion of this stage leads to the final and third stage of alchemy; however, it is more likely that this stage is on-going, but with less intensity, for the remainder of the life.

Re-View

In this chapter, we arrived at a paradox concerning women's psychological development. It can be regarded as a spiritual concern that is equal in its transformational value as a path of human love being embodied and lived out. The wild woman guides us to celebrate our innate human condition of embodied spirit, incarnation. We examined the role of suffering in a woman's individuation journey and looked at the Psyche and Eros myth as a guide through that suffering. Women come into relationship with masculine and feminine aspects—particularly the wild woman—in order to be vital in our humanness. That does not free a woman from suffering, though it does involve accepting of and relating to the archetypes in our psyches. Love of soul cannot be separated from human love, and both are part of the experience of the wild woman. And we discover that after much psychic excavation—and self-discovery—we are simply called to be.

CHAPTER 4
Relationship

"Some Kiss We Want"

There is some kiss we want with
our whole lives, the touch of

spirit on the body. Seawater
begs the pearl to break its shell. . . .

Close the language-door and

open the love-window. The moon
won't use the door, only the window.

Rumi, 2001, p. 125

How do wild women engage in relationships? There seems to be no definitive answer, no right or wrong way to be in relationships. There are no fixed rules for how wild women engage in relationships; however, a relationship is the alchemical vessel rather than the desired goal at the end of a personal metamorphosis. Perhaps the heat of being in a relationship is what causes the transformation rather than the belief that we transform and then engage in a relationship when we are flawless. A woman can choose a relatively simple, workaday companionship relationship rather than a big love relationship, which is a perfectly respectable path. However, many of us hope for a relationship that does not have to be one or the other; we hold out hope for transformative, passionate, intimate love that can be resolved into something simple, sweet, sustainable, and durable in day-to-day reality. It appears to be more the anomaly than the norm.

In this chapter, we explore the transformative aspects of relationship and the struggles that the soul seems compulsively drawn to. We explore this alchemical process through the lens of the wild woman, and we hold that compassionately. The wild woman's perspective is often in conflict with the "I"-ego perspective, a conflict at the source of much frustration. We look at how ego consciousness can develop a relationship to the wild woman, which is a *coniunctio* between consciousness and unconsciousness. Valuing that soul relationship contributes to creating conditions so that union may also occur externally. However, that cannot be the goal. Love of soul is the goal: an external love relationship can be the yearning, but it is not necessarily the goal; and therefore, there are no guarantees that as we engage in this process, the end result will be a worthy, wild man. Yet the wild woman in our dreams, other authors, and other wise, wild women who also esteem the value of love and soul encourage us forward with yearning as our guide.

Coming into relationship with soul is at the heart of the modern woman's transformation because the wild woman is culturally so mired in the patriarchal shadow. Coming into relationship with that emergent archetype is an undertaking essential to the transformative process. She gives hope for a sense of deep contentment and assuredness in oneself so that we may traverse the frozen dark tundra when that is what is in front of us or sit cozy by the fire when that is what is available. It is the harmony that arises from knowing we can trust the moment-to-moment consciousness of the wild woman and be responsive from a place of presence and embodiment. The *acceptance* of *what is* can bring harmony, whereas resistance often brings struggle and strife—accepting struggle and strife as necessary for the yearnings of one's soul seems to bring ease—and yet, paradoxically, we must often struggle to differentiate and move toward what soul loves and become conscious of her yearnings for love.

My hope is that there is a satisfying, sustainable, passionate, and intimate love available to wild women engaged with their own souls. I recognize that my hope for that outcome, which is only *one* possibility, is perhaps antithetical to the wild woman in her polyvalent ways. I see women around me creating a love that is engaged with their own soul, and it is possible for those of us hoping for it. The deeper value, though, is that relationship—in all its dissatisfied frustrations—can transform a woman and create a relationship to the wild woman.

This section is on relationship and addresses the following common questions that often remain unresolved paradoxes. *Once a woman has awakened, or become a conscious I, how then does she choose to relate? Does she become a we, which implies a merging of two? Can two people who are I's make a we? Do they want to? What would that possibly look like?* Ultimately, these questions wrestle with the paradox of separateness and togetherness, or autonomy and closeness. There is a dearth of literature about relationship for wild women. The Greek goddess of marriage, Hera, really belongs to the cultural dominant, and many of us do have a longing for a long-term, committed relationship—yet, one that is different from that which is modeled by Hera. She is the archetype of the jealous wife, often aroused by an avenging rage over her philandering husband, Zeus. We also want a relationship different from the dominant paradigm that, more often than not, ends in divorce—perhaps because of the archetypes or ghosts that, upon drawing two people together, subsequently cannot countenance the wild woman in the domestic arena, though this is where she is most needed.

Initial View

Hera is addressed in Downing's (1981) *The Goddess: Mythological Images of the Feminine*, Harding's (1970) *The Way of All Women*, and

Jean Shinoda Bolen's (1984) *Goddesses in Everywoman: Powerful Archetypes in Women's Lives*. Downing (1981) examined Hera by tracing back to that goddess's roots—prior to when she was seen through the lens of patriarchy. Hera was regarded as a complete female "pertinent to every stage of a woman's life: . . . maiden, wife, and also woman on the other side of marriage, woman separated from her spouse, woman as widow or divorcée" (p. 73). Downing goes on to explore Hera's ambivalence toward marriage and the nature of both this "pull and resistance" (p. 75). This clarifies the role Hera plays in life after divorce. I was speaking to a woman friend about relationships when, without thought, I blurted out, "I may marry again, but I'll *never* be someone's wife again." What that means is that the dominant patriarchal vision of woman as wife has passed, however, commitment recognized by ceremony may be a part of my life again.

Robert Johnson's (1983) *We: Understanding the Psychology of Romantic Love* examines the myth of Tristan and Iseult, which is arguably a retelling of Eros and Psyche and is an example of the powerful cultural paradigm of the suffering and impossibility of romantic love. The author argues that we must ultimately find the beloved within and learn to love the divine in the person we are with by not projecting the divine love onto the other. Moore's (1994) *Soul Mates: Honoring the Mysteries of Love and Relationship* looks at love through the lens of soul, stating, "The heart is a mystery—not a puzzle to be solved" (xi). Moore's work reframes relationship and the paradox of closeness and separateness by acknowledging that paradox is at the core of all relationship struggles and needs to be held consciously. In lived experience that means making the effort to be conscious of the compromises each is making and to be creative and patient while striving for fair compromise that is equalized over time. In *The Symbolic Quest: Basic Concepts of Analytical Psychology*, Edward Whitmont (1969) writes on the Eros function as "a relationship of mutual creative involvement and understanding, of distance as well as nearness" (p. 175). Whitmont directly addresses the paradox as well. Jungian Aldo Carotenuto (1989) in his book *Eros and Pathos: Shades of Love and Suffering* validates the passionate experience of love—for both joy and destruction—while still honoring that we must each do our inner work. Rollo May (1969), in *Love and Will*, argues, "Love cannot grow without Passion. The passion of Eros" (pp. 64-65). These perspectives support the ideal that a wild woman need not sacrifice passion in her relationship. Many relationships end unhappily because one or both partners end up bored and disconnected from the other once the passion leaves.

Carol Gilligan (2002) follows the Eros and Psyche myth in *The Birth of Pleasure: A New Map of Love*. Pleasure is the name given to the girl-child whom Psyche births after her journey is complete and she is reunited with Eros. Gilligan's work is about love, and the author makes an intriguing link to preadolescent girls whereby she recognizes that many females trusted their instincts before adolescence. This is connected to an unconscious state of *participation mystique* that I think actually extends into early adulthood for most women.

The lighthearted and playful book *Quirkyalone: A Manifesto for Uncompromising Romantics* by Sasha Cagen (2004) addresses the balance between independence and togetherness in a particular type of modern person—namely, the "quirkyalone." Such men and women (women primarily) "are the ones who don't have the option of camouflaging their individuality: they're just uncontrollably themselves" (p. 5). These women are independent, yet they also value deep love and intimacy, "preferring the thoughtful quiet of solitude to a depthless togetherness" (p. 101). Quirkyalones do partner in what Cagen coins as *quirkytogether*.

> At the core, quirkytogether values the idea of two fully formed human beings coming together for a partnership rather than a merging of souls—it's not the soul mate idea of finding the other half to complete you, but about finding a lively dynamic partnership that still allows you to be fully yourself. (p. 88)

This is an ideal that may also suit other wild women. It recognizes the instinct to partner and have deeply authentic intimacy while still maintaining sovereignty and separateness. My critique of this delightful book is that she addresses primarily people younger than 30 years of age, in whom I do not believe consciousness has had a chance to adequately develop. Further, if the maternal instinct grabs hold, many women who were previously autonomous and who fit the definition of *quirkyalone* do later merge with a partner, get pulled unconsciously into the dominant paradigm, and lose much of their previous individuality. After children, these women may wonder what happened to their lives and may complain about their husbands. I suspect it is these women who become among the 73% that end their marriages. As well, the ideal of "two fully formed human beings" is perhaps a lifelong goal rather than an achievable end in itself. Nevertheless, this book is inspiring by describing a way to consciously balance two individuals in a partnership—or two *I*'s that form a *we*.

I have spoken of the ghosts of the past that represent the puritanical voice of culture and have looked at some of Harding's work throughout; however, at this point, Harding actually represents one of those puritanical ghost voices. Harding (1970) holds marriage in high regard, arguing that it should be taken seriously. She speaks to the "old code" of marriage as "tottering to its fall" and contrasts it to the liberal and free ideas that cause women to have to "straddle the split between two cultural attitudes" (p. 220). She argues that there are "hundreds of women who want to eat their cake and have it too. They want the security which the old marriage code gave, but they also want the pleasure and excitement which the freer conventions of the day permit" (pp. 219-220). This divide is certainly part of the struggle; we women, nearly 60-years later, do want both the secure attachment and the pleasure and excitement. Settling for a "stirring the oatmeal" (p. 196) kind of love described by Johnson (1983) in *We: Understanding the Psychology of Romantic Love* just sounds bland and unappealing. So, the struggle continues.

Wild Motherhood, Feminine Feminists, and the Old Paradigm

Although we can potentially come into relationship with the wild woman at any age or stage in life, many of us women find that it occurs around midlife—usually after childbearing has shaken us awake. Aside from childbearing, any number of events may have caused the ground to fall out from under a woman. Maybe it was a little annoying mouse in the bed that kept nipping at her. Maybe it was a great shark from the depths. Or maybe it was a bear. The patriarchal system is failing. It is failing mothers, and it is failing families.

Little wonder that I want to leave this social construct and retreat to a Nicaraguan beach to be a surf yogini. On one level, before having my child, I was unencumbered and had the freedom of mobility to disappear. However, the thought of not having my son is insufferable; the price would have been too high. It would be a great failing of the system if the younger women coming behind us sacrifice the opportunity for motherhood because of impossible cultural pressures. The responsibilities heaped upon us women after we have children can make us feel hopeless; families implode. My fantasy is to be a surf-yogini-mama in Nicaragua *with* my son. I do not want my son to be raised in a system in which families have to contend with already impossible economic and social responsibilities. Many of us want to leave the patriarchal system entirely (of course that does not work practically for most of us). How can we women live in this culture but simultaneously not be constrained or domesticated by it? That tension is essential for discovering the path that each woman must carve out for herself. As single mothers in inequitable social and economic situations, we do have an endless load of duty and responsibility, and yet, this incredible tension is essential so that each woman can discover her unique path. There is nothing like having a child to keep a woman grounded and anchored to her earthly existence so that she does not fly off into heady illusions. Occasionally, there are women who cannot hold the tension, and they opt to leave their children. This is one of the most tragic signs that the system is failing women and families.

The feminist movement has been invaluable in creating options for women. However, women's equality is limited to equality within a patriarchal purview. Women as equals to men involves climbing corporate ladders, earning equal pay, enjoying equal partitioning of the work involved in homemaking and other responsibilities. The truth is these ideals have not been achieved particularly for women who become mothers. The *intention* of the feminist movement may be better expressed as women's right to be wild *feminine* women—*feminine* being equal to *masculine* as well as *women* being equal to *men*. How can we wild women be *feminine feminists*? How can we express our right to be feminine: unclear, submissive, passive, receptive, chaotic, sublime, lunar, sexual, adventurous, playful, creative, embodied, emotive, pluralistic, and maternal? The economic and social pressures on wild mothers whether partnered or single make it a near impossible reality. How can we be feminine without the misuse or abuse of women or the soul?

The problem lies in being captive to the system. How can we wild mothers leave the system without having to leave our family or our country? We can hold the tensions, with some awareness that the problem in the existing paradigm is bigger than our individual relationships and families, and we can trust that the wild woman archetype is gestating some sort of solution for us. In the spirit of *living* the wild woman's feminine energy, we wild women can wait patiently, receptively, intuitively, instinctively, and submissively for her, trusting that she—who is greater than we—is birthing a transcendent function in our individual lives and in our collective culture. She will guide us, and we will know when and how to respond. And it will be unique for each of us. Some will find ways to earn more income in fewer hours or ways to pursue creative interests. We each have a unique gift, talent, and purpose to bring into being, and we are all creative wild women who are capable of courageously manifesting our uniquely handmade lives—our greatest creation.

At a personal level, the stage of disillusionment with the cultural system can be seen in a generative light as an initiation into the second half of life—where life can become *one's own* life: unique, beautiful, glorious, and, hopefully, unabashedly one's own precious life. Although that is exciting, it is also tremendously scary. Most egos have enjoyed a sense of safety and control by doing what was always done, so the ego will come up with all manner of wily tricks to keep power and identity as the status quo. However, the price to be paid can be one's relationship to one's soul. The wild woman is surging in an uprush of feminine instinct in women everywhere, and we are all asunder, wondering which way is up. The romantic-relationship paradigm dominant in the West *maybe* used to work but no longer does. Now we have to feel our way in the dark, following bear tracks she has padded down in front of us. How do men and women relate in this new way? First, we have to learn how to relate to our own new, wild consciousness before we can hope to relate to another. More accurately, it is through relating to another that we can learn to relate to this aspect of ourselves. The ego relating to the wild woman is a wholly new paradigm for most of us. A wild woman in a romantic relationship is also a whole new paradigm.

Women at midlife are feeling an uprush and wondering what it means. Does it mean I should leave my marriage? Does it mean I should have an affair? What about the children? My husband had an affair; does it mean I should leave him? I do not love my husband, but he is the father of my children, so do I have to stay? We are a demographic that is poised on the edge of an old paradigm that is familiar, and therefore gives a false sense of safety and security, and on the cusp of a new paradigm that is bursting forth out of our dreams, full of passion and yearning, calling us into her dark forest and the unknown. We women who are experiencing the wild woman's emergence are strong, creative, and courageous, yet, until we engage with her, we may be overwhelmed with feelings of being controlled by our partners or confined by domesticity. Some do choose to leave marriages; others choose to commit more deeply to their own creative lives and personal intimacy without reliance on making external changes. Most of us were part of the cultural dominant of the traditional long-term committed, heterosexual, monogamous relationship—married either traditionally or by common law by cohabiting—and most of us have children. These are not the only women consciously engaged with the wild woman, though we are the women from that old tottering paradigm.

Those of us now single are asking: "What now? What does relationship look like now?" All manner of relationship shapes and sizes are emerging, and many women, after much work, are creating relationships that honor them. Most of us enjoy our freedom after feeling we were too domesticated and controlled or too well-behaved (and inauthentic) within the old paradigm of relationship. We may also yearn for a loving partner to create a relationship *differently* with us. First, we have to figure out what *differently* looks like (and I make a few suggestions in this chapter), or, if we do have a felt sense of what *differently* comprises, many of us have not found someone who can meet us there; the men seem more lost than we are. We are no longer naive young women. We are self-actualizing, we are grounded, and we have responsibilities; and we are looking for men (maybe women) to share life with, but we belong to ourselves, and our lives are ablaze with psyche. How to be in a partnered relationship that is in service to soul and love? What does that look like? It will be unique and evolving for each of us, but we look at some themes.

Love as the Alchemical Vessel

A few years after my divorce, I met my bear-man; I experienced our relationship as so-called big love—with the sweetness of first love but with depth, entanglements, and emotional complexity. More than any other, this relationship—with its agonizing frustrations, rejections, disappointments, and hurts—has burned me to the bone and transformed me. I have had to inquire deeply into who I am, what I want, what I value. It has brought me closer to the wild woman. This stage of longing for a male companion draws me deeper and deeper into relationship with psyche and all that resides within. The longing is an essential quality to soul-making. It is the longing that is both a transformer and the guidance toward the soul. Eventually, I had to accept that I will never have my wants, needs, and values met with this man; and stomping my feet, expecting him to show up the way I wanted (sexual and monogamous) was only making things worse for us both. As I could not will myself to fall *out* of love (though I put in a valiant effort), the challenge became: how can I love someone so deeply and still remain open to loving someone else? That was a new question for me and sidestepped the popular suggestion that the best way to get over someone is to meet someone else. I did in fact fall in love with someone else. The new man snuck into my heart as a no-strings-attached adventure, and because of that, I was able to let my guard down. The experience was intermittent over a few years and offered both sweetness and much shadowy exploration, and I could imagine a future with him. Falling in love with him was what snuck up on me, at which point he ended it in a way that felt cold and unrequited. Despite that experience, I still had not fallen out of love with the bear-man who remained in my life.

I am not a fan of the adage that if you let someone go, you make room for someone else to come in; that belongs to the monogamous paradigm of loving only one person. The wild woman is able to love more than one person. For a time, that led me to give consideration to the currently repopularized concept of polyamory, though I eventually concluded that I value deep intimacy, which does not seem prevalent in polyamorous relationships. In fact, it seemed like a way to tuck away, safe from the vulnerabilities of loving another and having to trust him. We can choose to be monogamous with someone because it is a personal value rather than an expectation as part of the mainstream model of relationship. Like a butterfly that alights on a fingertip, she lands with grace simply because she did, not because she was captured and a shiny ring was slipped over her wings, claiming her.

We can come to recognize the personified wild woman of the soul through loving another. The external journey is actually the catalyst for the internal journey, and one mirrors the other. The wild woman is embodied; therefore, her love is meant to be lived and experienced. Her love is not meant to be confined to our meditation cushions in our inner worlds; that would deny the relatedness that is central to her form of love. Woodman (1990) also wrote on the necessity to relate to both the inner and outer worlds.

> If men and women are to be partners in the outer world, the foundations for that partnership must first be laid within themselves. As within, so without. Nothing can be achieved without, if the foundations are not firmly established within. (p. 13)

Allowing that transformation to occur on both the personal and transpersonal levels allows for a deepening engagement to soul. Human relationship more than anything else has transformed me and brought me into a conscious engagement with my soul. It can be the vessel through which we learn that we are so much more than a singular ego with all of our childlike wantings, yearnings, and expectations. Running headlong into love with another who has his own soul journey in life is enough to thwart any ego's agenda.

As we mature by recognizing the reality and independent personality and life of the soul, we can foster love that nourishes the soul rather than when we were naive and not yet very aware of the vast wilderness within and when we found ourselves in relationships that unconsciously conformed to the cultural-parental paradigm. No longer do we look for a mate to create the white-picket-fence dream, because we are no longer under that illusion of wholeness and happiness. Now we look for something that complements our soul journey. That is a courageous thing to live, because the journey of the soul is a journey of individuation, and that path includes suffering. It is the elected path of women seeking to be the best version of themselves. Wild women seeking relationships at this stage of life will welcome love brought by grace that helps us deepen our engagement with soul. Monika Wikman (2004) in *The Pregnant Darkness: Alchemy and the Rebirth of Consciousness* suggested, "The person we can usually dwell with is the person we can individuate with and, at the same time, engage in the mysteries of love" (p. 167). Knowing that individuation with love is a challenging road fraught with unknown difficulties and uncertainties, we can better endure if we stay engaged with the wild woman of the soul in a daily way (through creative expression; embodied exercise like hiking, yoga, surfing, or dream work; active imagination; relating to nature; and so on).

In addition, as Hillman so often suggested, we must tend our often-not-pretty pathologies. In fact, our pathologies, Hillman argued in an interview with Laura Pozzo (1983), are *necessary* for loving.

> You are being made by the desire in your own bedrock, which is, of course, nothing else than your complexes, your problems, your unalterable bedrock pathologies. That's where the heat is and that's also where the increase of love is going on. (p. 191)

We must tend the relationships of both our inner world *and* our outer world if we are to invite the third presence—love—to remain and increase. One such pathology Hillman touched on is jealousy and its importance in making "you awfully conscious of the third"—the third, which is love, but not a personal love; rather, a love that "stirs the soul and generates imagination" (p. 186).

This third mysterious thing that we talk about regarding relationship is an essential ingredient; in part, it is the relationship itself as its own living entity, and both partners must tend that with care. Nathan Schwartz-Salant (1998) in *The Mystery of Human Relationship: Alchemy and the Transformation of the Self* describes that third thing as the space between the two.

> The true mystery of relationship lies less in the quest for
> understanding who is projecting what on to whom and
> more in the exploration of 'third areas,' the 'in between'
> realm which was the main focus of ancient science in
> general and of alchemy in particular. (pp. x-xi)

The ultimate gold of relationship is in its very mucky struggles that we run up against with one another, as each effort we make enables us to blossom more fully into our own being. Of course love is not *all* struggle; otherwise, we would never desire it. It is also the "divine ray" as Sappho (trans. 2002) wrote. Love is an archetypal experience that brings us into relationship with the transpersonal other; it can transport us into the realm of the divine—and it can transform us into humble-noble human beings.

The issue of possessiveness can be central to the transformative process. Personally, I was torn between wanting to be possessed and not wanting to be—between wanting to be possessive of my partner and wanting to honor his simply not allowing himself to be possessed, which was intolerable and created incredible tension and paradox within me. I had to look at my own icky, sticky possessiveness and desire for belonging to another.

In *Love's Executioner*, Irvin Yalom (1989) wrote about possession (versus possessiveness) in a case study of a 70-year-old woman in an obsessive compulsion with a man she had had a 28-day affair with eight years earlier. Yalom wrote about the fantasy:

> [he] provided you the opportunity to escape the pain of
> being separate and offered you the bliss of selfless merger.
> . . . The lonely *I* ecstatically dissolving into the *we*. . . . It's
> the common denominator of every form of bliss—
> romantic, sexual, political, religious, mystical. Everyone
> wants and welcomes this blissful merger. (pp. 26-27)

The longing to be possessed by that which is greater than us and to dissolve into the bliss of the greater mystery is both blissful and terrifying. The ecstatic merger of two is the enticing elixir for the epidemic of loneliness in our culture. There is both a desire to merge into this blissful *we* and a fear of losing our separateness. In relationship, the tension of being both a *we* and an *I* is the paradox we must hold with an attitude of fluidity as we move into and out of both experiences. Fluidity in that paradox feels authentic and possible. Nevertheless, the reason my relationship supported my individuation (and not my desires) is that my partner would not let me merge, so I had to stay a self-reflective *I*. For that period, it was what I *needed* for my individuation, though it was not what I *wanted*. The relationship ultimately kept putting me back on myself, having to take more responsibility for myself, forcing me into greater and greater self-reflection, and forcing me to wrestle with the only paradigm of love and relationship that I was familiar with. I had to re-view everything I knew about loving myself and another. In making meaning out of our individual experiences of struggle, we make the suffering endurable and valuable to our personal expansion—in other words, we make our lemonade.

Marion Woodman (1985) wrote on the issue of possessiveness in a mature love relationship.

> Neither is attempting to possess the other, neither wishes to be possessed. The relationship itself is unburdened by the pressure of needs and expectations. The partners do not demand a "whole" relationship, nor do they seek to be made whole by it; rather they value the relationship as a container in which is reflected the wholeness they seek in themselves. Each is free to be authentic. Living in the *now*, unfettered by collective ideas of how either should act or be, they have no way of knowing how such a relationship will develop. (pp. 152-153)

This is the ideal; even Woodman acknowledges it "sounds idealistic" but calls it "bedrock reality" (p. 153). There is concern, in that this ideal strives for perfection, and I am not sure a relationship can ever fully achieve becoming completely "unburdened by the pressures of needs and expectations." Perhaps in couples who have been together for fifty years, we may see that, but it is not reflective of my demographic focus of this book. The art is to remain in the flow or sway of moving between being free as an unpossessed separate being and being an intimate, interconnected part of a together-bond. As we mature, we become better able to be in that sway. A relationship that the wild woman is part of invites us to live in the *now* and is largely unfettered by collective ideas; it is unique to the bond that has formed.

Possessiveness is a mostly unconscious attempt to create or hold on to security: "If you do not leave me, nothing will change, and I will feel safe and secure," says the childlike ego. However, as we mature, we come to terms with the reality that we never know what will happen in life. There is no such security in a relationship, or a job, or anything. Security can never come from another but only from our own ability to trust ourselves to know how to respond in each moment to each situation as it arises. Even marriage vows taken in earnest do not preclude a partner from leaving; even the most conservative and stalwart may be tempted away. There is no way to know how long someone will be in our lives or to know why, when, or how that some-one may leave, but trying to hold on to the person with controlling behavior will not work. It will have the reverse effect and push the other away, yet—and so important—we must, again and again if necessary, open ourselves to trusting a different person and loving and being loved; otherwise, we harden, and life becomes a living death. Lao Tzu (trans. 1998) in *Tao Te Ching* offered the following wisdom on the perfection and interconnectedness of the universe, or Tao, but it applies to people too: "If you try to change it, you will ruin it. Try to hold it, and you will lose it" (p. 29). This speaks to trying to possess and capture another.

Possessiveness is not love, because "love claims no rights" (Castillejo, 1973, p. 127). Possessiveness and possession, although natural, are anchored in hubristic thinking, as though we can or are entitled to control and claim another person. In letting go of the old paradigm of relationship, we also have to recognize that love is fleeting and does not last, and we must grieve. When love alights, it is magic, and we can do our best to patiently await its return; recognizing the ebbs and flows of love, we can even strive to create conditions that will invite its return to the same relationship. However, there is absolutely nothing we can do to hold on to it, to capture it, to make it stay and continue illuminating our lives in a golden hue. If we try to capture love by trying to capture our partner and vice versa, love will most assuredly wither. Ironically, the most loving thing we can do is allow the other to follow an individual path—and to be allowed to follow our own path. In being given our freedom and in giving freedom, we create conditions wherein love may deepen—or return if it has flown off for a time.

Jealousy is different from possessiveness—we may feel jealous but not be possessive. Jealousy may be a very appropriate response to the grief of losing someone to someone else; it is when we try to be possessive and controlling of another that we are acting from a place that is fruitless—and harmful to love. Jealousy is a particular kind of loss—or imagined loss. Although most of us would *strongly* prefer to not look into our own shadows and deal with uncomfortable feelings of jealousy, it is necessary. This is an archetypal experience that belongs both to Hera as the jealous wife and to Aphrodite, who is green-eyed about anyone who does not worship her as the most beloved. As archetypal experiences, these affects are not going to go away. We can only learn to ride out the intense emotions, seeing them as separate from ourselves, not being reactive, but waiting to be responsive, and accepting that this particular quality of suffering is part of the human condition.

It is horrible when we are in it, feeling jealous or rejected. Jealousy is possibly my most painful emotional state and brings up feelings of not being wanted, which root in the soil of my birth. I was the result of an unplanned pregnancy for which my young and newly-dating parents were not ready. Rejection stings me deeply because I did not feel that my own being was recognized by my father as I grew into girlhood; rather, I felt I was the carrier of his illusory anima. The emotional affect associated with jealousy floods me with feelings of inadequacy and not being wanted and not being good enough, and it is torturous. I have dreamt of being victimized in Nazi concentration camps at such times. Irene Claremont de Castillejo (1973) in *Knowing Woman: A Feminine Psychology* writes about jealousy:

> Jealousy is not necessarily a mere egotistical desire to possess for one's very own, not just a selfish unwillingness to share. It is the anguish of despair; the wholeness one thought one had found with the loved one is shattered. . . . It is burning with intensity of one's desire for wholeness and one's desolation at its betrayal. . . . But if jealousy can be made to see; if a capacity and willingness to understand dwell in the heart at the same time as one is torn to shreds by jealousy, then the agony of despair can be lifted to another plane where its white heat can fuse again the scattered pieces of the golden coin; can make possible the return of love through acceptance of one's desolation and the humility of forgiveness. Wholeness is restored, but this time the wholeness is within the sufferer [her]himself. Dark jealousy, though often base, must not be despised. Rather let us beware when jealousy is absent. It smacks danger-ously of indifference. (pp. 128-129)

Jealousy, although immensely painful, has a rightful place in love and in life; it is often a great catalyst for awakening. Castillejo normalizes this immensely difficult emotion and further gives value to it by differentiating it from indifference, which is perhaps the coldest emotion and void of capacity for empathy. Indifference is the negation of love. In relationships in my 20s, I was not indifferent, but I was much less emotionally available. I did not allow anyone to be emotionally close enough to hurt me in that way; that depth was simply inaccessible, probably even to myself at that naive age. As we reach midlife, we are probably, for the first time as adults, able to really give and receive love, and thus jealousy shows up in ways it never had before.

To love another is to continually face the possibility of loss, which inevitably leads to knowing jealousy; and to know jealousy is to suffer. Suffering awakens us. Aldo Carotenuto (1989) in *Eros and Pathos: Shades of Love and Suffering* argues:

> We must allow for the possibility of feeling jealous and we must permit ourselves to experience it to the hilt. And this means to make the shadow conscious. It is wrong to think that jealousy can be overcome through will power. (p. 74)

The bringing of jealous suffering to conscious awareness is a way to remove projections on another whom we may have previously deified. Now we can begin to recognize that other as human and therefore imperfect or, better said, perfectly imperfect. We become mature enough to recognize our own pettiness and neediness. Jealousy is a way to become more related to our own vulnerable, imperfect humanness— and the embodied wild woman.

If we have been betrayed and our nightmare of losing our other to someone else is realized, we are given an opportunity, with time and through the pain, to move into our hearts and learn the art of forgiveness of both self and the other. There is only one way to learn forgiveness, and that is through trust broken by the experience of betrayal. Pathologizing is present to the extent that pathos is never split from the pathways of heart and soul. "Pathologizing is a hermeneutic which leads events into meaning. Only when things fall apart do they open up into new meanings" (Hillman, 1976, p. 111). The meaningfulness of pathologized events, such as betrayal, opens us to various stages of consciousness that would otherwise be unavailable—as if it were even possible to remain in the garden of primal trust. It is through suffering that we mature and the soul develops—"the salt of bitterness transformed into the salt of wisdom" (Hillman, 2005, p. 210). Once we find meaningfulness from the betrayal, we expand and deepen ourselves; we become more-varied and more-complex women who are rich and robust, strong and pliant.

It is important that as women we lean into the pathos (the Greek word for suffering) and let it break us open. Buddhist author Pema Chödrön (2000) in *When Things Fall Apart: Heart Advice for Difficult Times* suggests, like Hillman, that we allow pathos to open us:

> The idea of karma is that you continually get the teachings that you need to open your heart. To the degree that you didn't understand in the past how to stop protecting your soft spot, how to stop armoring your heart, you're given this gift of teachings in the form of your life, to give you everything you need to open further. (p. 111)

Although suffering from betrayal in love is something most of us probably work hard to avoid, it is a life experience that deepens us, builds character, and can make life more meaningful. Learning to forgive teaches us to open our hearts and build inner security while remaining soft. "Neither trust nor forgiveness could be fully realized without betrayal. Betrayal is the dark side of both, giving them both meaning, making them both possible" (Hillman, 2005, p. 210). Forgiveness comes from the openhearted place that is experienced beyond ego. In that light, the question of good and evil becomes a moot point, because all pathologizing then has the possibility of soul-making. The assessment of good and evil, and all the either-or problems of the monotheistic fantasy become irrelevant because we have made it meaningful. However, to realize this possibility of soul-making, love is necessary if the psyche is to develop through suffering. Maybe all we can really do is recognize love as an initiation of the soul—that the creative connecting function of Eros is awakening the psyche. From the perspective of *love of soul*, I can better endure the pains of impossible, frustrated, and seemingly unrequited love, recognizing that it is my love of my own soul that is awakening within and without in my life.

Personifying and Projections

Projection is an important aspect of women's psychological development of the animus. Let us explore projection in relation to Hillman's notion of "personifying" as a necessary aspect of the development of human relationship. In *Re-Visioning Psychology*, Hillman (1976) defines personifying as "imagining things in a personal form so that we can find access to them with our hearts. Imagining with the heart refers to a mode of perception that penetrates through names and physical appearances to a personified interior image, from the heart to the heart" (p. 14). Personifying is the way of viewing the complexes and archetypal core at the center of the complex that gives form to them as valid autonomous entities existing within the imaginal realm. It is a spontaneous experience, and it regards the configurations of existence as actual psychic presences. Personifying is a way of soul-making; these imaginary persons are just as they are, which are valid psychological subjects with wills and feelings like ours but not reducible to ours; they are autonomous entities—or spirits, as other traditions may describe them.

"Personification," as opposed to personifying, on the other hand, is egocentric and identifies those persons as "resultant of mine, their animation derived from my breath" (p. 2). "It implies a human being who creates Gods in human likeness. . . . These Gods depict his own needs; they are his projections" (p. 12). I endeavor to maintain Hillman's differentiated use of *personifying* versus *personification*, and truth be told, I occasionally conflate the terms; but I earnestly aim to not conflate the *point* and thereby become unconsciously identified with these archetypal presences. I strive to regard all of them as autonomous guests, including the wild woman, though she and I are quite merged in our love affair most of the time. Personification is a term that can be interchanged with projection and is different than relating to an archetypal presence through personifying or applying an image to the presence.

The phenomenon of erotic projection is an example of where we find the gods in our lives today. "Personifying, having been dismissed from consciousness, returns surreptitiously as personalizing. . . . For persons are no longer just human beings; they have been dehumanized by being divinized" (Hillman, 1976, pp. 46-47). In other words, we see human beings through our projections rather than interact with the archetypal presence through imagination. This is complicated because on one hand, we cannot fall in love without projection. On the other hand, there is a real risk of not being able to develop a human relationship because the other may carry too much in the projection, causing someone to fall in and out of love repeatedly. My bear-man is also a two-time Olympian, and I have to consider that my projection initially was personalizing, whereby I was unconsciously deifying him versus seeing the human. The symbolic reading of falling in love with an Olympian—after all, Mount Olympus was the mythological home of the Greek gods—is not lost on me. My bear-man also represented the drive to be the best version of myself and actualize my latent potential, which he had accessed in himself. This was an aspect of the projection that I was entirely unconscious of until a year or two after the grip of the complex had released. Projection seems to peel off in layers, like a potent dream that we gain more understanding from even years later.

Here is a little story of initiating projection that captures the lived-out ritual so poetically. Von Franz (1980b) in *The Psychological Meaning of Redemption Motifs in Fairytales* tells the following story about the Bushmen of the Kalahari Desert.

If a young man is interested in a girl he makes a little bow and arrow. The Bushmen can store fat in their behinds, which stick out, and they can live on this fat in hard times. The young man shoots the arrow into that part of the girl's body. She takes it out and looks to see who has shot it; if she accepts the young man's attentions she goes to him and hands him back the arrow, but if not, she takes the arrow and breaks it and stamps on it. They still use Cupid's arrow! You see why Cupid, the god of love in antiquity, had a bow and arrow!

We can interpret the arrow psychologically as a projection, or projectile. If I project my animus onto a man it is as though part of my psychic energy would flow towards that man and at the same time I would feel attracted to him. This acts like an arrow, an amount of psychic energy which is very pointed. It suddenly establishes a connection. The arrow of the Bushmen of the Kalahari Desert says to the girl, "My anima libido has fallen on you," and she accepts it or not. But she does not keep the arrow, she brings it back; i.e., *he has to take back the projection, but through it a human relationship has been established* [emphasis added]. (p. 71)

This is a charming story. We see that the projection, or projectile, can be both literal and psychological, as well as conscious or unconscious. The symbolic action of physically shooting a projectile and the woman's response to it actually serve to create a ritual and consciousness around the action which is very effective. Such ritual would help us manage our projections, though in practice, most of us would not take well to an arrow in the buttocks. Also, what if *we* wanted to be the ones to shoot the arrow? Can wild women do that? Absolutely. But again, it is more than a little socially awkward.

For us Western, non-Bushmen who do not have such rituals, withdrawing projections, although necessary, is not done as easily as removing an arrow. Woodman (1985) wrote: "Withdrawing projections is invariably the most painful task. We fear the realization that we are essentially alone" (p. 153). That notion speaks to Yalom's idea of desiring to be possessed so that we can be in a blissful merger of a *we*, and yet in order to create conditions for love to enter our lives, not only do we have to become aware of our aloneness; we also have to love ourselves. From there we can build loving community around us, and perhaps romantic love and deep intimacy will grace us.

Yes, part of the process includes removing projections, however, we do not want to be dismissive of love by calling it a projection—as though it were an inferior process. Projection just is. It is a natural phenomenon that is our way of seeing ourselves in the world; it is not inferior. However, in the past, I too have been dismissive of love, thinking of it as an inferior projection because I was overwhelmed by it when it came.

> The miracle of being in love is too overwhelming an experience ever to be dismissed as a projection. I do not believe for one moment that a projection can in itself light up the whole world. It is the love which goes with it that lights the world. (Castillejo, 1973, p. 118)

In the past, I have carried the lamp of consciousness into Eros's chamber. I have had a tendency to be aware of the projective nature of attraction. I then strive to name my projections and have been unable to surrender to the experience without *analyzing* it. This is sad and can be detrimental to the foundation of a relationship. What is required is to be embodied more and not analyze at all. We can strive to simply listen to our partner's dreams, gaze unanalytically at his photographs, or take in whatever creative work he is sharing. To bring the lamp to such soulful encounters is destructive to the man's soul expression and shuts down any connection we could enjoy in his vulnerable sharing.

I had a dream about staying in the soft light of consciousness.

I am with a new, attractive man; we have been getting to know each other, and we exchange a deeply loving gaze. We are not ready to unite sexually, but I know that when we do, he will cherish me. We are on the grass in the far north, but all the snow has melted and the sunlight is bright and hot. We keep shuffling out of the harsh light of the sun and deeper under the branches of a big old apple tree that shelters us comfortably.

Feminine light is a soft, reflecting light—a gentle light. The shade of the archetypal tree (or Self symbol) kept inviting us to get closer and closer as we shared an erotic gaze. This is the realm of consciousness where love can flourish.

As with us women, the men are also striving to increase their self-awareness and not operate unconsciously from the dominant cultural perspective. Men want to find their ways to be more authentic and the best version of themselves as well. When I originally drafted this section, I titled it *Aloof Men,* but that never sat quite right because that is the model of emotional unavailability or indifference from which they are trying to break free. Men all around us are breaking ground by defining a new way of being masculine, and that includes being aware of their emotional and inner life and speaking up for that, just as we do.

Culturally, heroes are icons made from the big screen or in the sports arena, and historically, idealized masculinity was portrayed as emotionally aloof. Even Harrison Ford in the iconic Indiana Jones series in the early '80s was arguably less aloof than the heroes of modern-day equivalents such as Robert Downey Jr. as Ironman. But it is changing, and new TV shows, such as *The Flash,* show men hugging and telling one another they love them. The old, aloof model is socialized within patriarchal values and is not congruent with human nature. Referring to such aloof men in *Love and Will* Rollo May (1969) wrote that this image of the Western male in the popularized "masculine" role is that of "a suave, detached, self-assured bachelor, who regards the girl as a 'Playboy accessory' like items in his fashionable dress" (p. 58). May adds that this is because of the repressed fear of involvement with women, and argues that the underlying fear is repressed anxiety about impotence. Noninvolvement (like playing it cool), then is elevated into the ideal model. May's noninvolvement is the same as love's nemesis: indifference. May's work is quite dated, and it is that image of "playing it cool" from which modern men are actively freeing themselves .

As modern women striving for mature love relationships, we can feel frustrated. As men work on reengaging with their inner wild man archetype, the *too cool* can still come out. Men can struggle to identify and articulate their feelings leaving us perplexed. It is effort to change the cultural water because much of popular culture continues to perpetuate the image of a detached masculine. Brave men are rising to the challenge. Men's groups, podcasts, and conversations are popping up that contribute to defining the new masculinity. In my clinical practice, men vulnerably explore how to create what it is that they really want, which is of course the same as what we want: *deep intimacy and connection.*

Many women also fear attachment to someone else, but that may cause us to resign ourselves to a life without meaningful relationships; maybe the pain of disappointed expectations is too great, or maybe the overwhelm is too much. They refuse to risk falling in love 'yet again.' But individuation cannot occur without relationship. We are all vulnerable to that disappointment, and it takes tremendous courage to love again after heartbreak. However, most of us so highly value relationship and connection that we cannot help ourselves. Men, too, are sensitive to the vulnerable pain of being brokenhearted. It may be even more difficult for them because patriarchy sees that vulnerability as weakness and therefore demasculinizing, which is the last thing men want. It is a tragic double wounding, and modern men have to work hard at not becoming guarded fortresses. We women must also support our men in carrying the hope for the new type of masculinity that is emerging.

As we wild women and wild men are practicing more-authentic ways of being in the world, we are simultaneously creating new models of relationship as we actively deconstruct the old ones. In *The Birth of Pleasure: A New Map of Love*, Carol Gilligan (2002) explored with a couple in therapy the couple's relationship that had complicated into a love triangle consisting of the woman, her husband, and her lover after the woman's husband had hit her.

> Her beauty, her independence of spirit, her vibrancy, which drew him to her in the first place, now threatened him because of their power to draw other men as well. . . . What Phil loved most in Sonya, he tried to squelch, hitting her, trying to beat the life out of her, in a paradoxical effort to keep her for himself. (p. 59)

This is possessiveness at its worst: resorting to violence to dominate and control the beloved. In that case study, this was the catalyst that opened the door for the couple to work deeply and engage in open dialogue to move toward creating a nurturing relationship rather than a controlling, constricting one. The woman, Sonya, described the new paradigm she imagined for their marriage, which resonates for many modern women.

> Being present, caring about what's going on with the family and with me. . . . It's just the shift in attitude. . . . I really wish we could be best friends. That's what I think a marriage—a happy marriage—should be . . . and a friendship to me is a mutual thing. (p. 58)

The complexity, however, is authentic and not resolved cleanly. The couple continues to struggle toward the realization of the risk of loving: "If I love you, will you leave me? It is a child's question: if you leave me, how will I survive? It is every lover's question—the question at the heart of this triangle" (p. 61). That triangle is seen from the perspective of the man's being the one who risks losing his beloved; however, the risk goes both ways with men who triangulate their relationships. Phil (in this story) had to deal with his jealousy, which brought out in him the "struggle with the meaning of manhood: whether manhood and the courage of manhood require him to defend his honor and uphold the hierarchy, or whether being a man means having the courage to open his heart and express his love" (p. 63). These are difficult struggles when the culture still predominantly supports the detached model of masculinity. Men and women reshaping culture and definitions of masculinity and femininity are moving into a new paradigm that supports both men and women in having the courage to love—and to express it.

That story ends there and the questions remain unanswered. This is where we stand, holding these questions, because, ultimately, with the emergent consciousness of the wild woman, there are no guarantees or answers to: *What is going to happen*? We can only respond to what *is* happening. Love is risky: we might get hurt beyond what we think we can bear—and we might find out we can bear it; or, more likely, we might find out we cannot—and thus we are transformed. We might have to face what Phil called the "ultimate nightmare—one's woman in the arms of another man" (Gilligan, 2002, p. 60). This works both ways for those of us who have concluded that our personal values include monogamy. Leaving patriarchy for love or democracy sounds easy, even inviting, but it is psychically as well as politically risky; at least at first, it seems to mean giving up power and control. It does mean giving up power and control over another entirely. In doing so, love can flourish, whether in a home or in a nation. Gilligan refers to the myth of Eros and Psyche as a map for love and life and learning Psyche's seemingly impossible tasks.

> Sort, practically on an unconscious level; find economic sustenance, learn how to move safely in the face of danger, pay attention to the cadences of emotional life; take water, go to the source, repair relationships, know what you know; listen to the stirrings of nature, remember culture, face mortality and choose life. (p. 232)

Choosing life is equal to choosing love and vice versa. Love is the purpose of life. These are important parts of a new paradigm: choosing life and love, risking opening our hearts to another. Risking being broken open. Respecting the mutual courage to move into uncertainty.

A Circle of Love

We are by now becoming quite aware of the patriarchal model of society that we are in and all of the ways it affects us as women. Being aware of it gives us the opportunity to evolve it and set us free from its unconscious grip on our psyches. In *Communion: The Female Search for Love*, Gloria Jean Watkins (2002), also known by her pen name, *bell hooks*, advocates for love as a way to change patriarchy. However, we must consider that desiring to change the system before the system is ready to change is just as fruitless and hopeless as expecting a man to be emotionally available before he is ready to be. Change can rarely be imposed on another—whether an individual or a culture—yet the agitation is required in order to heighten the tension and move toward something more equitable. Maybe all we can really change is ourselves. One woman at a time advocating for love is enough to make a difference. In the meantime, we must learn how to live in the culture and not be dominated by it, that means becoming conscious of the way it effects our inner life and choices.

hooks is an optimist and a pragmatic realist about love. She has found that men who are emotionally responsible enough to engage with women as their emotional equals—in intimacy and in the bedroom—are in short supply. "Patriarchal thinking has socialized males to believe that their manhood is affirmed when they are emotionally withholding" (2002, p. 97). But there are men who are rising to the challenge and also want to know love, but to do so, they must be prepared to challenge patriarchy and its affirmation of power and masculinity as asserted through emotional aloofness or indifference. Those men seeking love are around us; they are the ones we should be looking for; and the "female search for love is what life should be all about . . . [because] genuine love will always lead us to be more fully who we are" (pp. 157-158).

hooks suggests that women write a practical list of hoped-for qualities in order to be clear about our desires and that we be more judicious about the men we decide to partner with.

> I was way past thirty before I made that useful list of qualities I most desired in a partner. Had I applied this standard of evaluation, I would not have chosen the three talented, attractive men who had been my serious partners before I made this list. They were, all three, liars. (p. 176)

Well, that particular little tidbit of wisdom has not worked for me; I have written more than one of those lists, and as a little ritual, I have even burned the papers I wrote the lists on to send them into the universe, but that has not magically made the love of an emotionally available man find me. Nevertheless, it is the search that matters because it helps us clarify our personal values and ideals so that we can know ourselves better and make suitable assessments. As Castillejo (1973) writes, "love happens" (p. 116); it is mystery. We cannot make it happen. We can only prepare the soil so that it can occur.

hooks's work helps me understand why I am drawn to the puer types—the ones who live their lives as nonconformists and who challenge patriarchy. She quite rightly suggests that "looking for love and looking for a man are two very different agendas . . . and guess what? Men are easy to find" (p. 159). So it is. Women looking for a companion need not be single very long. Women looking for love tread a surprisingly lonely path, because the one we really get to know is ourselves, until eventually, we find, we are in love with our own lives. At that point, we would not easily compromise our joy for mediocre companionship nor re-engage in situations in which we are dominated. Ironically, though, as we love our lives and ourselves, we can also feel more open than ever to shared love with another; but that love must have a quality of grounded patience rather than the embarrassing, desperate longing. As we come to self-love and inner security, the men we are attracted to and the men we attract are simply different from before. Our conduct is different as we meet another. We know ourselves and we speak up for our wants and needs. We have healthy boundaries, and we teach people to treat us with kindness and respect. As self-love increases, engagement with the soul is the deeper fulfillment rather than finding love in a relationship, which may or may not happen and may not even continue to be desirable.

Just as we must develop and have healthy relationships with women, we also have to learn how to have healthy friendships with men—especially men who are redefining masculinity and working at new models of relationship. Some of the men we encounter are expressing themselves and their emotions in many ways beyond words. They are painting, taking up photography, foraging for mushrooms, selecting sustainable food, teaching and practicing yoga, opting for vocations that are sensitive to Earth, and living communally with others. It is important for women and men to have these friendships—not as lovers but as friends, even though there may often be erotic attraction in at least one direction. In those friendships, we gain the ability to form sincere and lasting relationships with attractive men, and we learn to not sexualize the dynamic. Some of the friendships sneak up on us; as time passes, maybe we did not even realize they were developing.

Holding the tension of the erotic attraction has value and can release creative energy. It is easy to mistakenly believe it is best expressed in the bedroom, but that may dissipate the creative energy available, and the friendship or project you may be engaged in will not often endure nor is it likely that romantic love can blossom. These friendships can prove more valuable than if they were sexual. Sex is good, but women looking for love, who have struggled with misconstruing sexual interest as a path to love, may find fostering friendships with attractive men to be a nourishing path. At the very least, the erotic tension can be creative, playful, and fun; and the caring and mutual respect are special gifts.

We can be in a primary monogamous relationship, but we can still have healthy, well-boundaried friendships so that one person does not have to meet all of the other's needs. Perhaps we will choose to have more than one significant male relationship in our lives, and perhaps our primary partner will have other female friends. Maybe we can imagine several close friendships and a mutual monogamous primary partnership as part of a circle of love.

I apprenticed in shamanic journeying for several years, and during one particular ceremony, I was told I would have "many loves, because it is love that heals; but there would be one significant partner." At the time, I was so entrenched in the patriarchal, traditional model of love as an exclusive pairing rather than a communal circle that I shuddered at the thought; it created an insecurity in me that I did not want to bring into a relationship. It fed the fear that he might leave me if he grew close to someone else. That childlike fear ultimately created a possessiveness. Yes, we can tell our partner we feel insecure, and we should communicate that if true. But from a different perspective, a circle of loving relationships is a way of spreading love into the world.

Loving is also a way of subverting patriarchy: "Women who learn to love represent the greatest threat to the patriarchal status quo" (hooks, 2002, p. 89). Women have a right to be feminine feminists who are empowered in their loving. In fact, being feminine and embracing our desire to love is a courageous and valuable path any wild woman can be called to follow. hooks warns, "By failing to love, women make it clear that it is more vital to their existence to have the approval and support of men than it is to love" (p. 89). More of us are preferring to spend time alone, to get to know ourselves, to love our bodies, and to love our femininity while we remain patiently expectant in our search for abiding love. We prefer to love our lives while we search for love rather than settle for "finding a man."

In our search for love, we can learn of its many faces outside the one model of relationship into which we were socialized. We can also see women engaging in the resurrection of the Victorian notion of romantic friendships for both same-sex friends and a gay individual and friend of the opposite sex. Those relationships, although erotic, are not sexual and are often commitments that last a lifetime and provide a place where a woman can know lasting love. For example, two women may choose to cohabitate together, behave like exclusive partners, engage in emotional intimacy, though not be physically intimate. Although the relationships may transform, the two people are committed to the longevity of the relationship. This has also now become an emerging possibility for heterosexual men and women as more and more individuals and couples open their hearts to the realization that one person cannot be everything to another person. Perhaps Hera's wrath or Aphrodite's jealousy will creep in, but as we become more responsible with our emotions (the archetypal affects), we can learn to hold and feel the possessiveness or jealousy but *not* be reactive from that place, which is destructive to love.

Expanding our hearts in a circle of love, by creating a community or network of loving friendships can be a model for many women. The boundaries of each of those pairings will depend upon the people in the relationship. Our hearts can grow and expand, it does not need to be exclusive to one person; we can have multiple committed bonds. hooks calls these romantic friendships that comprise a circle of love. Whether or not it includes a romantic partner, an expanded circle creates community and communion. The commitments depend on the agreements of each relationship: perhaps there is no primary relationship, perhaps there is, perhaps there is monogamy (one lover), perhaps more, perhaps none.

The journey to selfhood can be an agonizingly lonely one; however, we can be alone together in a circle of primary relationships that support and sustain us as we journey. The circle is a place to give and receive love, although we may also continue our search for love. When we find a romantic love partner to whom we make a long-term commitment, the other relationships are enhanced and may transform, but the joy from each of the relationships is shared. That expanded circle resonates more authentically for me than does the non-monogamous model of polyamory, wherein it seems love and sexuality get conflated in practice, even though, as the word suggests, *poly* is rooted in Greek for *many* or *several*, and *amor* is rooted in Latin for *love*, not *lovers*.

Women can have a preoccupation with love, and it is nothing to be ashamed of. When it is absent from our lives we can be preoccupied with it, but we cannot magically create it. In her musings on love, Castillejo (1973) asserts: "Love happens. It is a miracle that happens by grace. We have no control over it. It happens. It comes, it lights our lives, and very often it departs. We can never make it happen nor make it stay" (p. 116). Love is a gift or blessing when it finds us. We do have some choice about whether or not we are going to show up for the experience, for the meeting of the other; but even then, it is only a small amount of choice—and a great disservice to the soul to waste love's invitation by not heeding the call. It is questionable about whether or not we "learn" to love. We go through the messy process of withdrawing our projections certainly, and we learn to understand one another, but that is different than learning to love. Castillejo does allow that we can perhaps learn to prepare ourselves for love: "To me it is a [wo]man's task, his [or her] greatest task, not to learn to love, but to learn how to create the conditions in which love can alight upon us and can remain with us" (p. 125). This is a life purpose calling: *to learn how to create the conditions in which love can alight upon us and can remain with us.*

Here are some clues to create the conditions for love to find us: recognizing the uniqueness of each relationship, remaining faithful to it, and holding the paradox of mutual service without betraying oneself, and not presuming to know what the other needs. The faithful following of one's own path toward greater love, wholeness and self-consciousness, while maintaining willingness to serve a partner, is likely to also meet the need of the partner. "Wholeness is both the goal and the key. Consciousness is the tool" (Castillejo, p. 124). Although I shy away from the image of wholeness as something achievable, and I even shy away from the pursuit of consciousness, what she is suggesting here, which is actually congruent with the Psyche and Eros myth, is that wholeness, consciousness, and love are all inextricably linked and in service to creating the conditions within which love can alight upon us and hopefully remain.

The role of the animus in relationships becomes challenging. Castillejo advises women to keep the animus out of relationships.

> The animus is indeed woman's faculty to separate, not unite; which is why, if she is trying to make a relationship as a woman, she had better keep this analytical separating part of her well out of the situation or he will wreck it with his impersonal, collective character. (p. 170)

That certainly confounds the problem. Being too analytical about the relationship as it unfolds rather than just being in it can destroy it. It is arguable whether or not those qualities are inherent to the animus or whether the animus in some of us may have co-opted them. Also, I suspect a positive animus relationship can support the woman developing a relationship and can mirror the external. Nevertheless, Logos, analysis, and a rational function that does separate—and that, on closer investigation, may not even be "rational" at all—are qualities of consciousness that are not helpful for relating and uniting. In fact, it is best to be conscious of that analytical quality of consciousness and ask it to step aside—or perhaps have the wild woman bare her teeth at him if necessary. *However*, being more discerning and discriminating when choosing a partner requires the ability to evaluate. We cannot be entirely selective about whom the arrow pierces, because love just simply happens. We are best off if we are patient and nurturing in letting love blossom and maybe if we are selective about whom we spend our time with, so that if love does alight, it is with someone who meets many of the qualities on our practical list.

During the writing of this section, I had a dream about the power of love to heal. The dream:

I have been elected to occupy the queen's chamber in the palace. It seems that because I was given her chamber, I am now queen of the palace. I have a woman friend who lives in a part of the palace and a male body-healer who comes to treat us. He is working on an old knee injury of mine and breaking down the constricting scar tissue. He visits regularly to treat us both. My friend also likes him, but with time and regular treatments, he and I become lovers, and the sex is raucous. Even in the dream, I am aware that being penetrated by a male is unusual for me, but we act with complete abandon. Post-coitus, I start to think and wonder whether this is complicated for him—treating both my friend and me—and her being attracted to him, too. It is not complicated for me. I inquire and learn it is not complicated for him, either. It gets complicated only if we think about it and make *it complicated; it really does not need to be.*

In the dream, I do not wonder whether it is complicated for my friend; it seems that as long as she is receiving her treatments—which are erotic but nonsexual—everything is fine for her, too.

Initially, I am thrilled to be elected into the queen's chambers, though I am aware there is no king but, rather, this male healer who heals the body by breaking down old wounds. I understand him as a personification of love as healer. It also seems to speak to a more open circle of intimacy, in which I do not feel the need to be possessive by prohibiting the healer-lover from doing his work with other women, though he does not need to be a lover with other women. An important reflection in this dream is that I was happy because I was primary to him. In reality, I am not content if I am secondary or tertiary to the man I regard as my primary.

The dream is also a testament to the importance of creative life to the wild woman. When I procrastinate doing my creative work, which is deeply embodied in me, she sends me horrific dreams of my son going unconscious or being in danger and the like. When I respond to her and address her and say, "Yes, I heard you. I am returning," then we flow back into harmony, and her dreams reflect her pleasure. After this dream, I woke up with the moon and stars still in the sky, excited to return to the book where she and I meet.

Re-View

What kind of relationship does a wild woman want? She wants a relationship that changes her—perhaps despite the ego's resistance to that change. However, there is no right or wrong or one single way to imagine how that may manifest. For each unique woman there will be a unique relationship fit, and the acceptance in whatever way it presents is what matters. She is wild and not so interested in being well-behaved and conforming to masculine ideologies. Thank goodness, because through her presence, we can have hope for new models of relationships that can be in service to the equality of the *feminine* and bring greater harmony to women, men, families, and the Western culture.

Love is the *pharmakon*: both the poison and the cure. "For one human being to love another: that is perhaps the most difficult of all our tasks, the ultimate, the last test and proof, the work for which all other work is but preparation" (Rilke, 1975, p. 37). Being called to love starts a painful and joyful journey of self-discovery. The journey includes relating to another, not simply living it out in our inner worlds; and it includes passion, which is rooted in the Latin word for *suffer*— indeed the full range of our emotional, animal body. Romantic love is not only a projection of our inner world. It is a catalyst that can transform us. It can call us to the task of individuation, a journey that must be undertaken with courage. In relating to another, we also learn how to relate to the wild woman. The wild woman's way of loving another teaches us courage and how to ride the emotional waves, how to be secure in the unknown and uncertain, how to take responsibility for ourselves, and how to tolerate ambiguity and tension. We flow between closeness and autonomy; we learn about the creative life force; and, ultimately, we attempt to stand heart to heart with the source of the mystery, the Other. As more and more people open up to explore romantic love in different models, we will break out of the spell of the romantic tragedy we have been in since *Tristan and Iseult* of the twelfth century. The wild woman is breaking through, and individually and collectively, we can celebrate a love that is boundless and open. This is my vision: I am a hopeful romantic.

CHAPTER 5
Sexuality

I talked with you in a dream, Aphrodite.

Sappho, trans. 2002, p. 32

Sexuality, like relationships, is an essentially interwoven part of women's psychological development. It is the last of the research chapters in this book because it has been the most difficult area of my life to claim as my own. Renewing virginity in the sense of becoming a woman who belongs to herself can be difficult because it is difficult to differentiate from the cultural view of women. Our sexual identity has long belonged to men and was defined through the lens of patriarchy. This is something Christine Downing (1992) in *Women's Mysteries: Toward a Poetics of Gender* also recognized.

> When coitus is identified as *the* sex act, it seems to follow that female sexual fulfillment *should* be found there. We don't always recognize the degree to which the emphasis on intercourse, orgasm, and heterosexuality represent a male model of sexuality, perhaps partly because many of us have been initiated into orgasmic sexuality by men. (p. 94)

Many women are *given* their sexuality through that male model, which separates us from our own fluid and personal experiences of our sexuality. By the time we reach the second half of life, we have an opportunity, through the individuation process and the awakening of the wild woman, to claim our sexuality as our own.

Many of us have sexual wounding and a hard time trusting Aphrodite—we are leery of her, of our own sexuality, and of male sexuality—and so we keep a fair distance from her realm in order to be self-preserving. My relationship to my own sexuality has vacillated between being within the precepts of cultural ideas of what is appropriate and acceptable, and exploratory and experimental. While many of us no longer believe in the illusion that marriage brings either security or wholeness, we can come to know our personal values after sexual exploration and reflection. After years of self-reflection, I still personally hold the values of heterosexual, monogamous, family life, though because that is not my case, I live with a circle of love. I know these are *my* values and not those imposed by culture because I have challenged them and explored them. They will not be every woman's values, and they will likely be fluid as a woman explores her sexuality and values.

Because I am not with a primary partner, I am in a position in which the need for physical intimacy is not being met. Sex outside of a pair-bond relationship is not a sacrilege; however, without a loving container, it rarely feels safe for me to be so vulnerable at this stage of life, and, worse, it can feel self-exploitive. This proves to be an unresolved paradox because I am not looking for a traditional husband-type of relationship, though I do want to expand my circle and create a family, albeit in a less traditional structure. Sexuality—including *frustrated* sexuality and love—definitely fuels the transformational fire, and that is the value in having the longing go unmet: it brings us into closer engagement with the soul. Also, frustrated sexuality teaches us how to control our compulsions, how to experience the alchemical sulfur, and not be overtaken by it. It is essential that we mature to the point to be able to manage our compulsivity—without its taking control of us—so that we can have nourishing relationships, especially if monogamy is the agreement with our partner.

Collectively, the wounding to the feminine shows up poignantly in sexuality—whether in the form of repressed sexuality, sexual abuse, or exploitation. The issue of sexuality is individual, sensitive, and complex, and the contrasexual archetype of one's personality is a valuable teacher and healer at best. Many of the texts we have had cursory looks at—and those we have examined in depth—also include sections on sexuality because the layers overlap and the texts on psychological development also address sexuality and relationships; those areas are of central importance to women's developmental process. Once a woman becomes more conscious of and more liberated from complexes and cultural expectations, her choices around her sexuality and relationships may change. This is the area of research that is perhaps the most complex in its subtleties. Once a woman is differentiating and beginning to express her sexuality on her own terms and as it is more fully expressed, it seems to move into a sensitive area. There are spoken and unspoken cultural *rules* about how a woman is to conduct her sexuality; men do not want an *easy* woman, as though the prize were an invitation into a woman's body. There is still the conflicting desire in women to be pursued and chased, to feel we are the prizes, which means we cannot be guilt-free when we give ourselves over in the moment if there has not been an appropriate courtship. Men, when they really like a woman, will not want to disrespect her by having sex with her too soon. There is some link between sex and respect, but it appears it is more of a deeply entrenched cultural belief rather than an authentic link for the individuals.

Sacred sexuality is fluid, and mostly it is embodied. It does not have to be a mysterious Tantric experience sourced from a foreign culture. It can also be simply meeting someone new, connecting, feeling the quality of Aphrodite's magic, and enjoying a full bottle of wine over an evening together that then culminates in consensual sexual union. Why is that any less sacred or less pure than going through a socially prescribed courtship before the first kiss? In fact, as soon as moralism and judgment come in—"Oh, I should not be doing this," based on those old ghost voices of the past—the purity gets sullied. It is the *moralism* that sullies, not the act of sexual union if both partners are present and attuned. If men are looking to have serious relationships with pure women who "do not give it away too easily," the purity of connection in the moment can get tarnished and the sacredness can be lost. That repression of the expression of female sexuality, paired with the conflicting objectification that we have in the West, has stemmed from Christian roots that seemed not to know how to adequately celebrate female sexuality, possibly because it is such a powerful force.

Many of us are confused about our sexual expression; we want to be free to sexually celebrate a fabulous connection with a partner, even if there has not been an adequate dating ritual. If Aphrodite's magic is present, gratitude is an appropriate response instead of guilt or shame, and we especially do not want to feel as if the man thinks we are too easy or not suitable for a serious relationship. It is a conundrum, and we have to be prepared to challenge certain cultural rules. It seems that creating a foundation for a "serious" relationship is a *different process* from celebrating Aphrodite in a connection that is not aspiring to be long-term. It may not be that either is more or less sacred, but discernment in the moment along with consciousness related to the powerful sex drive–instinct is what is required. There is a lack of literature that celebrates women's sexuality outside the cultural precepts. Because of that, the wild woman is the guide for this research through lived experience, reflection, active imagination, and dreams as well as anecdotes from couples and individuals who are living outside the cultural paradigm.

Initial View

Following are relevant texts that were consulted and considered in this research. Dossie Easton and Janet W. Hardy's (2009) book *The Ethical Slut: A Practical Guide to Polyamory, Open Relationships, and Other Adventures* "rethinks sex" and consciously examines beliefs provided by our culture. The authors have committed to non-mono-gamy, which is an option that may suit some women. Although that path suits some, it can also be a defense against the vulnerability of deep intimacy. My dreams on this topic concurred by guiding me out of the "complex called the open center" and suggested that the quality of openness in love that I was seeking had a more symbolic nature, akin to openheartedness. Nevertheless, the book is valuable. In addition to living outside the cultural paradigm, the authors write on jealousy as a path of spirituality.

> Jealousy can become your path, not only to healing old wounds but also to openheartedness—opening your heart to your loves and to yourself as you open your relationships to fit in all the love and sex and fulfillment that truly are available to you. (p. 130)

Jealousy is a powerful emotion that can guide us if we are willing to investigate the source of the affect. It can help teach us how to be with our painful emotional fears.

Individually, a woman must reclaim her own value in order to have a healthy relationship to her sexuality. Miranda Shaw (1994) in *Passionate Enlightenment: Women in Tantric Buddhism* argued, "When a woman reclaims her divine identity, she does not need to seek outer sources of approval, for a bottomless reservoir of self-esteem emanates from the depths of her own being" (p. 41). Tantra is, of course, an ancient paradigm, and there are many texts about it; it can be an expression of sexuality that is an alternative to the mainstream paradigm. In particular, Tantra offers a way for women to explore their sexuality as something to be celebrated rather than repressed. For many women in whom the wild woman is in shadow, in whom potent sexual instinct has been sullied, and in whom sex has been viewed as dirty or a power issue, Tantric practices may offer a way for them to reclaim their sexuality with confidence.

Aphrodite's Daughters: Women's Sexual Stories and the Journey of the Soul by Jalaja Bonheim (1997) is a compilation of women's sexual journeys. Bonheim approaches the sexual stories of women with the "belief that sex is an inherently sacred and soulful force" (p. 9). This lens is important to acknowledge because we must reconsider deeply what sacred sexuality means. Bonheim collected and shared several anecdotes from courageous women willing to share their sexual journeys. Her first story, belonging to a rotund woman called Roseanne, describes the aspiration for her work.

> Roseanne's story describes perfectly the transition we are all trying to make. Her two relationships have taken her from repression to liberation, from inequality to equality, and from sexual frustration to sexual fulfillment. She has done what women are collectively attempting to do, which is to leave the patriarchy behind and empower themselves to live in ways that honor the feminine spirit. (p. 34)

This is the simple and, of course, difficult goal of the work of individuation and differentiation from culture. The author goes on with Roseanne's story, and we find the invisible tracks of the wild woman that helped Roseanne make this transition.

> How did you learn to honor yourself? I am not sure, but something inside of me has always known. . . . Something within us knows, no matter what we were told, that our sexuality is neither sinful nor dirty but, on the contrary, miraculous and sacred. . . . Still, once this innate knowledge has been so thoroughly repressed, it usually takes a special key to unlock it. (pp. 36-37)

The "something within us" that Roseanne spoke of is related to the good instincts of the wild woman once they have been recovered from shadow. This tragic message that so many of us women bear with regard to our sexuality as *sinful* or *dirty* is precisely the message that brings shame, tarnishes the very sacredness of it, and deeply wounds us. This is just a small piece of one of the rich and fabulous stories in Bonheim's work.

Sexual Fluidity: Understanding Women's Love and Desire by Lisa M. Diamond (2008) explores the unique nature of women's sexuality at different times in their lives that is not in keeping with the cultural paradigm. Diamond's work is largely about the fluidity of female sexual orientation. She wrote:

> Sexual fluidity quite simply means situation-dependent flexibility in women's sexual responsiveness. This flexibility makes it possible for some women to experience desires for either men or women under certain circumstances, regardless of their overall sexual orientation. In other words, though women—like men—appear to be born with distinct sexual orientations, these orientations do not provide the last word on their sexual attractions and experiences. (p. 3)

Diamond's research in this area is important for women who are no longer constrained by the cultural paradigm and may find themselves surprisingly attracted to someone of the gender opposite the one they are usually attracted to. Many women leave the dominant heterosexual paradigm, then experience attraction or openness to a relationship with a woman; for some women it becomes more about the attractiveness of the *person* rather than the *gender*.

The more we come into relationship with the wild woman, the more fluid and less fixed all areas of our lives become—in particular, our sexuality. Diamond elaborates: "Some women will experience relatively stable patterns of love and desire throughout their lives, while others will not" (p. 10). It is a possibility that may present itself to women beyond their choice; it is unexpected and beyond their control. Because of this, her work highlights and normalizes this fluid experience that some women may experience, and hopefully, they do not suffer too much confusion, shame, or guilt for suddenly desiring to deviate from their familiar or dominant paradigm. In fact, woman are going beyond even the largely culturally accepted paradigm of labeling sexuality as lesbian, gay, or bisexual. Women are giving up identity labels because their sexuality does not fit an existing label. It remains personal and individual to the woman and is not a matter of taking her out of one box and placing her in another, which feels merely like an effort to contain the woman.

Claiming the Body After Separating

Many women separate from their animal body and its wisdom— usually fairly early in life and very often as the result of some degree of trauma that may or may not have been sexual. Therefore, before we can hope to find our own expression of our personal sexuality, we first have to recognize that split and then endeavor to bring awareness to the areas of wounding so that we can learn to hear, feel, and love our own body. The body carries the wisdom of the instincts; the wild woman communicates to us through our bodies and our dreams. Our bodies let us know when something just 'doesn't feel right.' But many of us are conditioned to ignore our body wisdom, we begin to discredit our instinctual knowing in favor of the mind. Rejection of the body often starts around puberty as a result of the messages we receive consciously and unconsciously from our parents. Just by virtue of living in a culture that portrays Eve as the seductress and as responsible for original sin, most of us have been wounded sexually; we received the confusing message that our bodies are both objects of desire and scorn.

We got our messages from the culture and from our parents. A young girl raised in a home where she received complex messages about her body and her sexuality may unconsciously perceive that her sexuality is there to serve males or that it is a power she dare not wield, lest she be viewed as a temptress and seductress, like her great grandmother Eve; or conversely, she may exploit her sexuality as power. As such, many young girls separated themselves from their bodies, instincts, feelings, intuitions, femininity, and sexuality. When the wild woman emerges, she wants to bring up those aspects from the depths so that a woman can claim what is rightfully hers: her ensouled, wild body wisdom. There are many confounded, complex reasons and ways a mother may have communicated negative body messages to her burgeoning daughter. The mother may not have felt feminine in her own body, because femininity has been negated for untold generations. Perhaps the mother unconsciously considered her daughter a rival for the father's attention, maybe out of envy of her daughter's youth, imagining her as more beautiful. Depending on the mother's personal history, she may have feared male sexuality herself and warned her daughter to hide her body. And she may have feared the powerful energy of her own sexuality and desires, which she could see developing in her adolescent daughter. All of those messages—and more—from a mother can inform a growing girl's experience of her own body and may have communicated to her that her body was something she would not want to be identified with. This creates the split or repression of body awareness in favor of messages provided by family and culture.

The father may have played an essential role, too. How he responded to his daughter's transformation dramatically affects how she responds in contrasexual relations and how she understands her own sexuality going forward. "A father's warmth, playfulness, and love are very important to a girl's healthy sexuality. . . . A father's dominance, possessiveness, and criticism can undermine or destroy a girl's heterosexual development" (Murdock, 1990, p. 43). We all hope fathers and father figures will be the guardians of a young girl's growing sexuality; however, that is not always the case. Many fathers simply do not know how to respond to their daughters' transformation, and there are few cultural models for positive father roles. One of his many roles is to fashion an atmosphere that affirms his daughter's developing sexuality. For a girl brought up by a father or other male authority figure who ignores his natural role as protector of his young daughter's sexuality, this will become a significant part of her individuation journey as a woman. She will have to claim her sexuality as her own and will have to learn she does have rights and how to exercise them.

Sexual trauma is tragically pervasive in our culture. Most women have sexual scarring. Women who experienced sexual trauma in early life typically separated from their bodies as a means of self-preservation. However, the body has its own intelligence and stores the memory of the trauma. Women will become numb and dissociate from the body to forget and not feel the humiliating pain associated with sexual trauma. But the body remembers and stores it. As a woman matures, and as her ego strength is fortified, she perhaps becomes more able to open up to discovery of those areas of her body where the wounding is stored. Maybe the wound is stored at the site of the physical wounding—a woman's vagina, cervix, breasts, hips, throat, and so on—though that may be too literal because the somatized affect is often highly symbolic and mysterious. In writing about women who suffer body separation through abuse, Murdock emphasizes the opportunity to turn the wounding into a healing gift.

> I have found that many of my clients who experienced sexual abuse at an early age either become incredibly sensitive body-workers or are totally out of touch with their physical limitation. They either turn the wounding into an experience of deep understanding of how pain and confusion are locked in the body and can be released, or they armor their poor wounded body, anesthetizing themselves to their own instincts and intuition. (p. 117)

This understanding offers women a way to reframe their experience into something positive and nurturing for themselves and others. Such women can become sensitive body-workers, and they are usually highly empathic and intuitive, but that gift can be applied to *any* vocational calling. Indeed, as women liberate their sexuality, their very presence seems to invite others to come home to their own bodies.

Depth psychology recognizes that the physical body mirrors and affects an individual's psyche. Bridging the psyche–soma split by inviting a mature woman to reconnect with her somatic wisdom is essential for woman to mine the jewel of her personal sexuality; her authentic expression of her sexuality is felt in her body, and therefore she must strive to stay present in her body. If we look to the soma as a messenger of soul in much the same way we would look to a dream, then hopefully, we can make choices that are in accord with a more holistic perspective that includes the embodied soul, the wild woman. From a depth psychology perspective, pain or suffering can be a doorway into a deeper complex, a symptom and can be seen as a gift. Psyche and soma are inextricably connected, and movement at one level necessitates awareness of change at the others too; consciousness then becomes grounded in praxis, and decisions are made from a somatically informed perspective. An energy block or injury to the psyche may present in the soma and vice versa. Awakening awareness in the body where sensation has been split off from consciousness due to trauma or violation helps to dissolve the blocks; this reconnects us to the organic life of feeling and can help heal the split between body, mind, and soul. As we become more embodied and awaken the split-off parts, we actively reclaim our bodies as our own and are also actively engaging with the wild woman whose wisdom is known through the body. The mind and body offer different modes of wisdom, and both are required; the key is to differentiate the various modes. Many of us sometimes find it just too emotionally painful to be present with the organic feeling life of the body. It takes tremendous courage to be at home in one's body and feel the full range of human experience: the love and ecstasy, the suffering and pain, and everything in between. It is a challenge to reclaim the wisdom of the body.

It is valuable to combine depth psychology with somatic work—such as yoga or dance—so as to open and release blocked parts of the body and come to new awareness and understanding. Consciousness is required in order to understand the *meanings* of bodily experiences, and integrate psychological levels of the process. Somatic work paired with psychotherapy can provide insight for the client and bring about a new perspective, which is required to integrate the bodily experience. Imagination and awareness can be helpful in making a particular symptom meaningful and in providing a new attitude and perspective. Psychotherapy can assist and support in that important integration step so that it does not fall back to the unconscious. But we want to not be too concerned with seeking *meaning* at this stage. That dishonors the emotional, non-reason-oriented soul by being analytical, literal, and rational—by relying on our Logos consciousness for meaning. However, we can honor the wild woman's symbolic language—without necessarily rationalizing it—by making an encounter with the numinous *other* that is embedded in the body *meaningful*. This is not always done easily, because we can slip into seeking clarity, but that is the *ego's* way, not the embodied *soul's*. As we become present to the ever-increasing subtleties of the body, we are invited into a heightened awareness of the moment through movement, feeling, and sensation. Awareness is key in shaping our experience, and indeed our very aliveness. It is a gift to be an embodied human; we are blessed to have this vessel to sense life. Somatic learning has the power to enhance the grace, beauty, and enjoyment of life. We all have a right to enjoy life. When we come to recognize the gift of being in a human body, we can savor all of it.

Another way to reclaim the body is to work with dreams. Dreams are pure unadulterated voices from the autonomous psyche, and like the body, hold innate wisdom to which our conscious self may not otherwise have access. Stephen Aizenstat (personal communication, 2010) highlighted that with the simple words, "The body is always dreaming." One of the techniques that Aizenstat taught for working with dreams is to embody the dream figure. In doing so, we begin to build a relationship with dream images. A dream about a tree, for example, means to stand like the tree and feel its deep roots penetrating the earth and the vast branches reaching skyward while the strong trunk provides home and shelter for all the guests. To physically stand in the pose of a tree and feel its beingness in one's body is to relate to the tree in a new way, and we may find that from that tree, profound emotional strength is available to us that can hold all of our concerns. Just a note of caution, however: this kind of work is best done in a supportive environment, because some dream images should not be embodied. These may be powerful symbols of archetypal forces that are not all benevolent. So we run the risk of overidentification or absorption if they are not related to with respect and care. Embodied women can trust their instincts about which dreams would lend support and be helpful to relate to through the body.

We become more embodied through attention to the immediacy of soma, through the opening of blocked areas with practices such as yoga, and through working with embodied dream images. As we do that work, we affect the psyche, and conversely, as we work with the psyche, we affect the body. Once we have made strides in inhabiting and reclaiming our body, we can move on to reclaiming our sexuality. This is not nearly as linear as I am making it sound; like all processes of the psyche, reconnecting psyche and soma will likely be circumambulating and probably disorienting. We can only strive to be present and aware of the body's messages.

Claiming Sexuality

What does a woman's authentic expression of her sexuality look like? This book starts from the premise that we get socialized into our experience of our sexuality, really from birth, whether or not we go through a direct experience of sexual trauma. The quickest way possible for a woman to know what is authentic for her is if she is connected to the immediate feedback of her own body: however, not all of us have such immediate access to our bodies. Downing (1992) suggests that discovering our own sexuality requires listening not only to our bodies but to our dreams and fantasies. For those of us who more readily relate to dreams and fantasies, this is a helpful invitation; reclaiming more directly the wisdom of the body can be a slower process. For example, I dated a fabulous man—one who sounded good on paper and one my mother would surely have delighted in. I was rationally thrilled. My body response time was not immediate, and it was even confusing and conflicting, because when he kissed me, I had initially responded with arousal. A fantasy image was the first to breakthrough to awareness, and this slipped out three times: "I feel like I am a butterfly and he wants to pin my wings to a corkboard." My friend—a soul companion and an art therapist who has known me for 30 years—gently said, "That sounds like it might feel really violating." It still took a few days to land before I could finally recognize that the fantasy was telling me what I had been slow to hear from my body: that this man, wonderful though he was, was not where my libido was pulled. Our bodies are hardwired for pleasure responses, and that can send confusing messages if it is also quietly telling us that something is just not right. Those of us whose body response time is in training and slower have available to us other soulful means of reflection: dreams, fantasy, and—with luck—dear and trusted friends.

Women's authentic expressions of sexuality is ever changing and renewing and always unique. What works for one woman will not work for all, and what works for one woman one time may not the next. This is so whether we are talking about such issues as vaginal orgasm versus clitoral orgasm or larger issues such as sexual orientation, which many now recognize is also changeable. We wild women are not easily pinned to corkboards. Female sexuality is slippery and fluid by nature. It requires the woman to be in a constant state of responsiveness to her own sexuality and to develop a relationship with her inner wild woman, who expresses herself in soma, dreams, fantasy, nature, and synchronicity too. We want to strive to respond to each erotic moment, exercising our rights to assert or decline or to explore or disengage from the other. Those of us who struggle to remain present and focused for a sustained period of time can simply fall back to taking space—whether a moment, a day, or a week. Our sexuality is ours to own, and we do not owe it to anyone to share it. Conversely, if we feel gripped by desire and attraction, we have an equal right to offer an opportunity for connectivity.

Along our journey of reclaiming our sexuality, we want to recognize the polyvalent nature of women. In keeping with the wild woman's moment-to-moment consciousness, we must recognize the undulating nature of sexuality and respond to how it is in that moment. When we receive our messages about our sexuality through a male cultural lens, we are more likely to be comfortable or inclined to accept that our sexuality is passive and receptive, that our vaginas are receptacles inviting penetration and offering pleasure in exchange. Yes, sometimes maybe we are passive and receptive, but at other times, our sexuality may be hungry and active; and we have a right to express it as such (of course, with consensuality underscoring every sexual encounter). A woman who has reclaimed—or is reclaiming—her body may find her sexual desires burn and find they are in conflict with the sexuality she was taught. Downing (1992) wrote:

> But once awakened to our own active desire, how quickly we learn the untruth in the old equation of activity with maleness, passivity with femaleness. There is so much in my sexuality that is not receptive, not primarily responsive, but active, initiative taking, hungry. In fact, there is much evidence to suggest that men have always known that and feared it, that the image of female passivity is counter-phobic, apotropaic. As indeed, the intensity of our desire, its rawness, its wildness, may also sometimes frighten us. (p. 95)

This is rich phrasing. For cultural reasons, it has served the patriarchal fantasy to allow and encourage women to be *typically feminine* in the bedroom, where we embody the qualities of passivity, receptivity, and meekness. However, as we attune to our fluid desires, we may redefine feminine to include qualities of aggression, unpredictability, and formidability.

Male sexuality dominates the bedrooms of the West even today, after the rise of the feminist movement. It serves men well. It serves patriarchy. It probably even serves most women insofar as they do not have to take responsibility for such a powerful force. While some men may encourage women to be more assertive in the bedroom, it is important for women to do so for their own desires and not to service their lover's desires unless it is truly reciprocal. A wild woman, even though she can be passive, receptive, and responsive, can also be a potent huntress who does not miss. She is the quintessential polyvalent representative of the full range of the feminine. She is the shape-shifter extraordinaire. And if she is ravenous, she will seek satiation. If she is languid, she will luxuriate in receiving her lover's offerings.

I approached this book with a question that emerged from a dream: Do wild women wear high heels? I could not make sense of the question. I floated it past a few women, who proved to be naysayers. One informed me, "No, because high heels were for tethering a woman to a man." Whereas I understood her to mean symbolically, it nevertheless seems to be historically inaccurate, because heels were originally for horsemen to hook on stirrups. Another said, "No, a wild woman would never wear anything to please a man—only to please herself." These were truths for those women at that time. For others it is: "If the mood was upon her, yes, she would, and she would sling her bow and quiver on her back before she went out with her lips shining." Downing wondered:

> Why in the world is wearing high heels associated with pleasing men? It can please us; it can please other women. In fact, I believe, many women (not only lesbians) mostly dress for other women—they notice more than men—of course it can partly be competitive not just to please. (C. Downing, personal communication, 2014)

The wild woman's expression of sexuality can be intense, raw, wild, and, perhaps at times, frightening. It can also be languid, receptive, and nurturing. A wild woman wears high heels and bare feet and everything in between—whatever she likes. She enjoys expressing her sexuality on her terms, for herself, for men, for other women, or just because.

Female Phallus

During the writing of this book, I had many potent dreams that were challenging to process and integrate. In three of them, I roared ferociously at a father figure's inappropriate, impotent attempts at seduction; I was no longer attempting to be polite and placating, and he withered in the face of my energy. Meanwhile, I also had visitations from a spectacular dream woman with a *female phallus*. She seems close to the moon goddess from the earlier dream, though more humanly accessible:

> *I am in a sexual foursome. My male partner is with me in the tangle of bodies, and I intend to perform oral sex on him. However, the phallus I discover is extraordinary; I discover it belongs to a beautiful woman with an elegant neck, an exquisite face, bright blue eyes, and short black hair in a pixie cut. I am positive I want to be with her. She and a third woman inform me of some consequence of that (which I willingly accepted in the dream but forgot what it was upon waking). Being in her presence inspires a feeling of love and awe like I have never known. She penetrates me, and both of us orgasm immediately. Then we kiss for a while, she penetrates me again, and we orgasm a second time.*

A few days later, I have a subsequent, related dream.

> *A man I am attracted to (in real life) is having dinner with the woman who penetrated me in the earlier dream. How could they know each other? It seems she is his girlfriend or they are in some form of a relationship at least. I begin to awaken, confused and sad, believing that neither is available to me. Then I hear her say, "Remember to expand your circle of love; if you seek only one love, you will have to keep repeating this lesson of rejection. One may become primarily significant, but only through maintaining an expanded circle."*

It is a complicated sequence. This hermaphroditic female with a potent phallus is such an enthralling figure. Other than knowing that the hermaphrodite is the offspring of Aphrodite and Hermes, I did not know much about hermaphroditic lore. Synchronistically, a book arrived in the mail, and it most conveniently fell open to a section on the hermaphrodite. In *Mirrors of the Self: Archetypal Images That Shape Your Life,* edited by Christine Downing (1991), is an essay by Jung, who wrote:

> The hermaphrodite means nothing less than a union of the strongest and most striking opposites. In the first place this union refers back to a primitive state of mind, a twilight where differences and contrasts were either barely separated or completely merged. With increasing clarity of consciousness, however, the opposites draw more and more distinctly and irreconcilably apart. If, therefore, the hermaphrodite were only a product of primitive non-differentiation, we would have to expect that it would soon be eliminated with increasing civilization. This is by no means the case; on the contrary, [wo]man's imagination has been preoccupied with this idea over and over again on the high and even highest levels of culture. (p. 158)

The hermaphrodite is not only an early form of nondifferentiation but also a symbol of the creative union of highly differentiated opposites. As a symbol, the hermaphrodite bridges between the unconscious substratum and the conscious mind, and it bridges the *present-day consciousness* (consciousness informed by culture) with the natural, unconscious, instinctive wholeness. Little wonder this figure is enamoring and fascinating.

How amazing to be penetrated by a feminine female with a robust penis. It is different from Dionysian bisexuality, because Dionysus is male. (I explore Dionysus in more detail later in this chapter.) It is similar in that both seem to be modes of bisexual hermaphroditic consciousness—neither wholly male nor wholly female but, rather, both. The dream woman is graceful and feminine, with a virile and potent phallus, and both feminine and masculine are present and powerful in her. To be the receptive lover of such a woman is an ecstatic experience. It seems there are consequences, one of which is the necessity of releasing the old paradigm of relationship with *one* person (in part, as represented by the impotent father figure dream sequence). There is a strong reiteration to create a circle of love (which may be the consequence I forgot in the first dream). I did not interpret that to mean multiple lovers or a Dionysian orgy, as symbolized in my dream, but more like the circle of love, wherein one person is not expected to meet all the needs of the other, though there is a primary partner.

If I consider the dream literally, perhaps I am still too resistant to the model of polyamory as meaning multiple sex partners and open relationships. The wild woman's way is poly*everything*: polyvalent, polytheistic, and polyamory, at least in the sense of multiple loves— why not polysexmates too? The difference is that I am imagining a *significant* sexual relationship that is *mono*gamous; that last remaining *mono-* is an attitude that has strengthened with time for me. So I accept it as my personal value, and that is fine. However, if I consider the dream symbolically, I can wonder who all these aspects are that I am currently intimate with psychologically. In the nature of this work there are multiple archetypes: the wild woman, Aphrodite, Artemis, Diony- sus, and so on. During the writing of this book, these are the lovers whom I was in a hot, sweaty tangle with. Each archetypal perspective offers a different way to view the questions and therefore offers different solutions available to us as well. The tension of polyamory versus monogamy can be viewed from any of the present archetypal attitudes. The nature of love is wild; it defies delimitation and requires continuous reassessment and response based on forces that are present in each moment.

The traditional definition of a conventional relationship was marked by whether or not sex was involved: if you were having sex, you were in a relationship. If it were a marriage, then sexual monogamy would be the hallmark of a traditional marriage partnership. Monogamy was often, inaccurately, called *fidelity*, and it had very clear boundaries: the parties agree to have sexual relations with no one else but each other. Clarity is comfortable. That is one of the great things about the traditional paradigm: everyone knew and understood the rules and had a sense of security in that knowing (albeit, often a false sense of security). Also, some give lip-service to the rules without actually following them. Affairs are as old as the institution of marriage and are very common because, *fortunately*, soul is not fond of such rules. And so one's conscious, culturally assumed values may be entirely incongruent with one's unique personal values, which may or may not be conscious. As well, the shadow will express itself somehow too. Perluss offered:

> If one's persona is based on a certain moral standard, and the shadow is denied, well, we know it will appear against the ego's will—somehow/somewhere. Being monogamous due to societal morality is very different than being monogamous because it's what feels right at the time. (B. Perluss, personal communication, 2014)

Soul is continuously inviting us to expand and open our hearts to love—a love that is, in the end, boundless. We cannot get there in one day; each new relationship she draws us into carries the invitation through its struggles to redefine what love is. We often face a choice: harden, defend, and uphold the old definitions and forms of relationship or surrender, sink in, and let the tides wash those lines away and open us further to an expanded love.

As those relationship forms change, so too does the most commonly looked-to way of defining relationship: sexuality. As the paradigms become less and less formed and structured, how is sexuality becoming expressed? My relationship with the bear-man, during the years when I was writing this had many expressions of love, except sex. In this way, the absence of sex could have defined our relationship—if

I had let it. From another perspective, I could have let what was present define it. Eros was present in the way we remained continuously connected even through great time and distance. Also, we remain committed to staying in each other's lives regardless of the other people who enter ours, though the relationship continues to change. Intimacy and emotional care were also present over shared meals, held hands, and loving gazes. Even bickering the way old couples do was sometimes present. What was absent were sex and exclusivity. Sex and exclusivity used to define relationship; however, *what is present* is at least as important and valuable as what is absent.

The role sex plays in women's new relationship paradigms is just as shape shifting as the relationships themselves. We are now invited to courageously reconsider how we define our sexuality. In *The Future of Love: The Power of the Soul in Intimate Relationships,* Daphne Rose Kingma (1998) explored the following questions.

> What will be the role of sex in the relationships of the future? Will it continue to be the main characteristic that defines a relationship as it always has in the past? Or will our relationships run wild across sexual boundaries in such a way as to make our sexual behavior meaningless? Since we are in the habit of using sex as the line of demarcation between what constitutes and what does not constitute an intimate relationship . . . the role of sex in our new unions will be of even greater importance. (p. 189)

If we are engaged with the wild woman, the role of sex may run wild across sexual boundaries, but it does not have to be meaningless or reckless at all. In fact, if we can stand at the crossroads and leave the well-trodden, maybe even paved, trail and follow the pull of our hearts into the trailless wilderness of the wild woman, it will be meaningful to the soul. Fidelity becomes redefined as being faithful to yourself, to what you believe, to whatever commitments you and the person you love have consciously decided to make. Fidelity is no longer connected to sexuality in this context—unless we make that choice. As we open the boundaries of what is comfortable for our relationships, new configurations of emotional intimacy will also create new meanings for our sexual commitments—we become free to choose what we want sex to mean. As we make the choice to follow the wild woman and embody soul, it gets scary and frustrating when our expectations are not met and we no longer know which direction to move in. It is those frustrations that can invite us to engage in the struggle that will expand our love; or we can dig in, resist, and hold on to the old way.

Years ago, when I was just beginning to understand there might be another way to love my partner beyond the conventional form—but before I understood that I was being invited into more-expanded soul love at the time—I had the following dream.

> *I am in an old town at night. I go into a saloon-type place where a young man has died, perhaps having been murdered. His body is covered, and people are tending to it. There is an old printing press, one of the first. I'm very excited by it and have knowledge of how to run it. It is in working condition and has even been updated. Both a male caretaker and I are ecstatic about the machine and appreciate all of its intricate parts. He tells me, "We now print on vinyl: it lasts forever." This press is only for very important writings. A matronly woman who is trying to maintain social order comes after me; with the caretaker's blessing, I take two of the page plates and flee with them. I escape to the ocean, where the waves wash over my feet, giving me a feeling of groundlessness and calm. It is night, but there is a golden light on the beach. I can see far down the lonely coastline, and there are so few people there.*

Aphrodite, in one myth, is born out of seafoam—the kind of water that washed over my feet and gave me a sense of the ground's washing away. In retrospect, this dream resembled a baptism by Aphrodite, whose light is also a golden light. This was perhaps the first glimpse I caught of Aphrodite in my dream world. I did not recognize her at the time, though I knew I was leaving the collective represented in the matronly woman. The heart path does have a feeling of groundlessness, and the ocean can come and wash all our lines away, creating a blurring of boundaries—a blurring that is necessary for the emergence of an expanded love and new expressions of sexuality. However, as we come to know our unique values—and ourselves—we must set healthy boundaries and speak up for what is okay and what is not okay in each moment, experience, and relationship.

As we begin to explore sexual energy from a new conscious perspective we venture into new territory, and learn more about what sexual energy *really* is, and discover our healthy boundaries and ecstatic possibilities. To explore that new terrain, we must remain attuned to our bodies, dreams, and fantasies as we feel our way forward in a dim golden light. Kingma (1998) wrote: "Boundaries draw lines. They don't bring us to the altar of kinship. They keep us at arm's length from love. . . . We need to relax, trust, and keep on tiptoeing across the boundaries, even though each little step may be frightening" (p. 195). We need to take just one little step at a time, breathe deeply, muster some courage, and then take the next step. We do not need to know more than each moment, but the journey is taking us toward a boundless soulful love, and the way there consists of one moment and one step at a time.

Dionysus is the god of women, wine, and ecstasy. He is responsible for confounding many boundaries, including the boundary between masculinity and femininity. Christine Downing (1993) in *Gods in Our Midst: Mythological Images of the Masculine: A Woman's View* discussed this god as *"pure libido"* and suggested we not necessarily think of him "in terms of unbridled sexuality, [but] as devoted to women—to their in-their-selfness, not their social personae" (p. 59). Therefore, this god belongs to this book because even though he is a masculine god, he is also potentially present for women who are engaged with the wild woman.

We might wonder why a male god is represented as having this power to bring women in touch with their instinctual nature. My sense is that this communicates that when women are among themselves, emancipated from the receptive and nurturing role expected of them in hetero-sexual contexts, they may discover an active sexuality that is their own, a sexuality that encompasses an obsessive insistence of its own expression. (pp. 59-60)

Dionysus is both an exciting and a frightening god—and largely in shadow, as his pure raw energy is a threat to the conventions of society and the narrow bonds of ego.

The maenads' frenzied orgies and dismemberments are terrifying images of being taken over by the god in a state of uncontained ecstatic bliss. He represents a wildness that threatens the dominant culture. His energy is the experience of our own instinctual energy and can be celebrated though the expression of solo sex—masturbation—as well as sex with others and through the intoxication of wine. His sexual instinct is different from Aphrodite's, which necessitates a pairing of two. Women coming to know their own sexuality and their bodies and can enjoy giving over to Dionysus through pleasuring their own bodies and exploring privately the secret erogenous zones that tease and that excite all forms of ecstasy. Through consciously experiencing Dionysus, we can escape mundane reality. But there is a warning with the power of that passionate energy: because he is *the vine*, there is a risk of becoming addicted to the substance, wine, rather than being able to hold a sacred place for him. He comes into the world of women as "the loosener, [which] is especially appealing in times when the burdens of autonomy and responsibility, of existence in the social world, seem too constraining" (Downing, 1993, pp. 65-66). As we women are opening and loosening the boundaries of roles, relationships, and sexuality, Dionysus is a welcome, and required, guest on our journeys.

An aspect of sexuality, with which I have more experience with than I would like to have, is in sublimation of libido. I use the term *libido* in keeping with Jung's more expansive definition, wherein it is understood as raw, creative, and psychic energy that can manifest as instinctual sex drive but does not necessarily. During the several years that I consider my peak period of individuation and transformation process—I experienced a *sexual awakening* however, with only limited opportunity to express it, the energy increased because it became frustrated. By *awakening*, I mean I became aware of my own sexual desires and body responses as a woman who was not driven by an unconscious instinct to seek a mate for protection, procreation, or husbandry. During those years, experiences were few and far between but included ecstatic dissolution; exploring darker, more shameful aspects of my sexuality; and, on the other extreme, ascetic practices—which included abstinence from any form of arousal, including in the dream realm.

That radically powerful energy burst into my life, had very limited sexual outlets, and, in becoming frustrated, intensified. That source of raw libido is the energy that sustained me through graduate school, through the creative process of doctoral dissertation writing, and through the fundamental period of the rebirth experience. It is the same energy that motivated me to get into my body and engage in physical exercise, which further increased vitality and libido but which also allowed the energy to move and flow rather than become blocked and stuck. It is the energy that found expression in the sensuous world of nature: the moistness by the river, the rough skin of the tree, the warm kiss of the sun, and the beat of the raven's wings. By sublimating that energy, I found deep intimacy in a bubbling stew and in sharing it over wine or in reorganizing the garage so that belongings could fit together and clutter be removed or in lighting candles and creating a close space. There were times that the energy was offered to spirit through prayer in seeking to create my own life in a way that was meaningful and openhearted.

There were also times that sublimation of sexual energy became "repressing" sexuality—and was wounding. However, from that I learned that my path is to embody and live my life and not retreat into the comfortable-for-me world of spirits. I learned to move between both worlds with some ease. Ultimately, the sublimation of sexual energy generated the libido for transformation and rebirth, but that is only *retrospectively*. *During* the process, it was painful because it was not what I wanted, which paradoxically was the catalyst for the transformation.

That understanding of the sublimation of sexual energy is ancient and is commonly heard of among spiritual seekers living as celibates. In *The Soul of Sex: Cultivating Life as an Act of Love,* Moore (1998) wrote about an expansive range of sexual expression in life. He expressed value of the erotic and sensual relatedness of objects. "A discussion of sexuality isn't complete unless it takes into account the extended erotic life of the objects, large and small, that fill our world and contribute immensely to our lives" (p. 241). He goes on to write of his relationships to his beloved piano and collection of books referring to such things as companions. For me, it might be my leather jacket that I like wrapped around me making me feel held, feminine and sexy. Though, importantly, this type of meaningful relatedness is different from neurotic materialism:

> If we are filling the emptiness of our lives with objects, we may do the same with sex. Developing a philosophy of life that regulates our acquisitiveness has a central place in getting our lives in order generally, and without that piece in place nothing else, including sex, will have a place. (p. 245)

We can understand that surrounding ourselves with things that hold value to the soul because they have quality are handmade perhaps, are beautiful, and inspire deep feeling. We can *ornament* the world in which we live as a way of expressing our feelings to the objects around us. In that way, we can inhabit and relate to a sensual, erotic, and sexual environment.

Pleasure, Play, Paradox, and Longing

Three days prior to writing this section, I was told about *Taboo: The Naughty but Nice Sex Show* in Vancouver, British Columbia. I went with a friend the next day. It was an expo of vendors selling various sex toys and costumes, women learning to pole dance, men performing strip teases, physicians talking about the numerous erogenous zones, a sadomasochism dungeon, and many booths in between. The whole atmosphere was imbued with a spirit of playfulness, openness, and nonjudgmental, sex-positive expressions. It was peopled by those of all ages and orientations, coupled or singled, friends or lovers, and men and women mostly in regular clothes but many in celebratory attire. It reminded me of the importance of playfulness in being sexual; after all, if we forget to giggle, how do we get through those moments of getting our skinny jeans off over our ankles or the various noises our bodies make? There was no need to be modest or bashful at this event; the speakers were open, funny, and informed; and they made it possible for everyone to feel at ease because of their own level of comfort. "Sex is nice and pleasure is good for you," is a theme in *The Ethical Slut: A Practical Guide to Polyamory, Open Relationships, and Other Adventures* (Easton & Hardy, 2009, p. 23). This attitude of sex positivism that erupted in the '70s was the spirit of the Taboo exposition.

Sex sometimes likes to be taboo; it can be the naughtiness that makes it arousing and erotic. The idea of the "naughtiness factor" was expressed in *The Erotic Mind: Unlocking the Inner Sources of Sexual Passion and Fulfillment* by Jack Morin (1995, p. 84). Morin advocates an understanding of a new paradigm of the erotic that is paradoxical in nature. "Many find it discomforting to tolerate ambiguity of the erotic experience, to accept its mixed motivations, or to observe how the erotic mind has a habit of transforming one idea or emotion into another" (p. 6). We want to understand our own erotic nature as vast and multifaceted. The paradoxical perspective is the only viewpoint large enough to encompass that truth. It is vast, multifaceted, mysterious, and complex. Holding paradox certainly helps accept the complexity of sexuality. We want to try to unearth the mystery of sexuality and understand our own eroticism while still holding paradox and allowing for unanswerable ambiguity.

When we engage with the wild woman and become more conscious of our sexuality, paradox and the conflicting aspects of oneself become evident. Our hearts want one thing and our instincts want another, while our ego is generally overwhelmed by desire or guilt, or is fighting for control. The more we individuate, the more life becomes full of paradoxes or contradictions that are frequently painful and appear beyond our control. Nothing takes us more directly into the fullness of life than these contradictions, particularly regarding sex, love and spirituality. Paradox and contradiction are not impediments but are in fact integral to our process of "becoming," and it is perhaps at those pivotal points that we are invited to respond by going further into the mysteries of life and creation. Our response to the paradoxes we are presented with invite us to living into the contradiction. We are not to "solve" the contradictions but, rather, move more deeply into them and allow them to take us further into the realms of the wild woman. From this place we are invited to open, expand, and transform.

Longing, like all acts of imagination, is soulful and highly selective, and imagination, of course, belongs to our fluffy-tailed friend. What is she saying to us through her selective longings?

Longing also has natural affiliations with romantic love. It's difficult to imagine the experience of limerence without the pre-occupation that fills the hours while lovers are apart. . . . [Once united, their joy is] usually short-lived. Soon new obstacles intervene so that yearning can continue. (Harris, 2007, p. 77)

The absence of the loved one is what stimulates longing, fantasy, and arousal. In fantasy, the imagery is naturally of fulfillment, but the arousal springs from longing. Longing is still more common among women than men and is associated with romance. Longing is hardly pleasurable—in fact, it can often involve intense suffering when it is believed to be for more than a short-term absence. However, it can also be a paradoxical experience of yearning for reconnection as a form of prolonged foreplay and energy buildup. Such arousal can then lead briefly to fulfillment before the connection is thwarted again and the longing cycle repeats. Foreplay is exactly what the word implies—play before—and *before* does not imply a subsequent goal (like orgasm). For women, foreplay is so important that it should nearly always be a part of intercourse. However, foreplay is not dependent upon intercourse. Anticipation and longing can become fused; anticipating seeing the loved one can definitely be a strong aphrodisiac, particularly if playful flirtations get communicated back and forth in the time of absence. The soul seems to naturally long for her love, as acts of suffering and passion. She also plays an essential role in longing as part of sexual fantasy and arousal.

Mirdad (2007) in *Sacred Sexuality: A Manual for Living Bliss* offered a contrary perspective on longing by arguing that the role of longing is the continued search for something *unfulfilled* within oneself; he does not explore the soul fantasy of fulfillment and arousal, and therefore his definition does not include the affects of the soul. He suggests that what we desire and long for is a union with God (he does not so much seem to mean "in the monotheistic, Christian sense" as he does to equate love with God). He argues that we eventually realize it is futile to displace our desires onto one person or to single out any one person as the object of our love, because love could be felt for all people and things. If we fixate our love on one person, that very person becomes the obstacle to our experiencing a God-like fluidity of loving consciousness. On monogamy, Mirdad wrote:

> Nevertheless, we can still choose to demonstrate a unique—even monogamous—love for one person . . . But even the most amazing monogamous relationship has its potential traps. For example, when a single person takes an exclusive place in our hearts, we tend to reach for that person with longing, which indicates that we perceive

something is missing within our own being. In such cases, love is no longer expansive and unconditional, but becomes contracted and fear-based, which always results in pain and suffering. (pp. 8-9)

Love is expansive, even if we choose to be monogamous; and longing can be a symbol of yearning for connection with the divine, though only in part. However, we never achieve a continuous state of either absence of longing in some form or an absence of pain and suffering. Life is just not static like that, nor should it be. We can simply try to be aware that longing is inescapable and is the soul's yearning for what she loves—whether divine love or, equally sacred, human love. Longing does not imply a perception that something is missing within our own being. Loving—and longing for love and connection—require someone else; this is a requirement of the soulful life, not a signal that something is missing within us. Human love is a way of expressing divine love, and the two are not separate. As we embrace our humanity and the full range of human emotion and experience, we *are* engaging in sacred practice. Sacred practice is not some God *out there*; it is expressed in each moment of our precious human lives.

We all know that sex can be separated from love and vice versa, and many have had or witnessed the experience of sex that leads to romantic love (or at least long-term relationship that was believed to be "love"). However, less commonly in our culture, the "opposite can also occur: romantic love can lead to sexual desire" (Diamond, 2008, p. 203). This is more common in women as sexual desire can develop for women in the way opposite to their usual sexual orientation. For example, a woman who has previously experienced her sexuality as heterosexual may find that her orientation changes into a sexual love for a woman for whom she earlier felt a strong platonic love. Diamond's point is that when there is strong Platonic love, it is possible for a relationship to change into a sexual one.

> This connection makes it possible to start out with strong platonic (that is non-sexual) feelings of love for another person, and sometimes develop new and unexpected sexual desires for that person. . . . This occurs because love and desire, despite being separate processes, nonetheless have strong cultural, psychological, and neurobiological links between them. (p. 203)

Sometimes we experience a relationship that began as a nonsexual friendship without so-called chemistry, until eventually, magically, Eros arrived. Then it can become also sexually fulfilling and grow into a nurturing and unique relationship for both partners. Although it may seem somewhat obvious or even logical, I personally know of only a very small number of instances of such a change, and the individuals had done a great deal of honest self-reflection prior to uniting fully. Perhaps it is just my demographic, for Downing observed that a move from friendship to a surprising, sexual relationship—and then even on to second marriages—may be "more common at midlife" (personal communication, 2014). These new experiences may become more frequent as we mature.

Reciprocal romantic love and sexual desire have remained split for me through the second half of life, and there is not much that can be done to change that. A true aspect of holding the tension of the opposites is that there is no solution. There really is not—just a new attitude toward the problem emerges. In holding the tension, I am invited to accept that romantic love and sexual experience have been disparate. Yet, I have loving, nonsexual relationships in my life, especially the maternal love of motherhood. Life is full with the responsibilities I have created, and that fullness is enough.

The wild woman invites us to celebrate the human condition of embodiment and the gift of being able to experience pleasure and joy with our sensual, sexual bodies. From the perspective of the wild woman and other archetypal figures such as Aphrodite, it is irreverent and disrespectful to deny the bodily pleasures if that is the energy that is present. In this polytheistic way, a new attitude toward sexual relationships is available. Although sex can still be pleasurable—and even sacred and transcendent at times—for many of us, sex without intimacy and connection, while maybe *hot,* is usually not fulfilling. Women place a high value on soul connection. For some of us the real orgasm may not be physical but emotional—the sense of being fully met by another. We experience a loss when the soul connection is absent. What we value most about sexual ecstasy is the feeling of being in touch with the sacred—as the body mirrors the soul, the most intense body experience is also the most profound soul experience. We need to feel intimate connection with our partners. In addition, we do well to remember to play, be spontaneous, greet fantasy, accept longing, be open and nonjudgmental, and enjoy the profound ecstatic pleasure possible with our bodies. These are invitations only; women's sexuality need not be constrained and have limits, because whatever feels integral for each woman in each moment is ultimately that to which we want to express our fidelity. In this, we make room for a soulful expression of sexuality that is fulfilling to a whole woman, including her body and her deep being.

Sacred Sexuality

Female sexuality is a beautifully complex mystery. Fear of the unknown is intricately woven into sexual expression for most women— fear of losing control because we are invited to surrender ego control and consciousness during sexual encounter whether alone or together. At its core, sexual fear is, perhaps, a fear of being overtaken by the divine—a fear of the realization of our own smallness. Simultaneously, that idea also constitutes the drive and the longing in sexuality: the union of the human with the divine in a moment of fleeting, transcendent, ecstatic bliss.

Some women are able to easily give themselves over to sexual play and seduction and the enjoyment of multiple nights of lovemaking and pleasure with little effort. One friend has been referred to as Marilyn

Monroe numerous times and even Aphrodite herself. She seems to be able to embody the great goddess in the temple of her home and the temple of her body with ease. And, like Monroe, a significant shadow causes her to suffer intensely at times as well. Women at midlife, whether single or married, may be dissatisfied sexually. Although most of us believe we have glimpsed *sacred sexuality*, it has not been often or with ease. The definition of sacred sexuality that I offer here is by Michael Mirdad (2007) in *Sacred Sexuality: A Manual for Living Bliss*.

> Sacred sexuality is about sharing and exploring an intimate relationship with this inner spaciousness beyond the dense, material body. It's a state of living in vibration of the soul. . . . Technically, all sex is sacred, as are all souls, but not everyone treats it that way. Nevertheless, irresponsible use of sexuality does not remove the sacredness but merely veils our ability to see and experience it. . . . [Because] the word *sacred* refers to "the spirit" and *sexuality* refers to "the body," the two words combined describe a merging of the worlds of spirit and matter, or soul with the body. Sacred sexuality is about experiencing levels of ecstatic bliss and unconditional love. (p. 2)

From the perspective of the wild woman, all sex is sacred. Mirdad's work borrows from many ancient traditions in sexuality and combines them to relate to modern, lived experience in the West. He distinguishes between sexual depths and sexual heights, suggesting that *great sex* is often connected with heights and that it focuses mainly on stimulation of the nervous system. However, it can in fact be a "dance with her demons" (p. 12), even though the woman is attempting to access and release her repressed sexual emotions. This is when a woman is acting out of her wounding, or exploring dark, shadow aspects of her sexuality for which she carries shame. Such women mistake something "special" about an *edgy* relationship because they get so aroused. But some of that *specialness* and orgasmic energy comes from unseen levels of emotion that get triggered and need to be released.

Mirdad describes two types of sexual experience generally: the first focuses on the 'heights of sex,' often referred to as great sex, whereas the second he describes as the 'depths' of sex. Sacred sexuality accesses the depths and the soul; it encourages deep emotions and motivates people to reach for their hearts. On the other hand, sexual heights focus on hot intensity and quantity of stimulation and the success of orgasms. What is commonly called *great sex* usually does not occur with established partners or mates, but with someone with whom there is little or no emotional investment. By great sex, he is here referring to sex that is intense, hot, exciting—bigger, better, louder, harder, faster, more. His point is that *truly* great sex involves the depths, which is a sustainable warm or cool energy, though depth of sex may also include the experiences of the heights, but as a secondary priority and without the need, goal, and obsession for such.

This is a separation between the heart and the pelvis, of spirit from body, and of love from sex. For sex to be truly great, it must have true depth and genuine feelings of love and caring. Heights are more commonly sought and experienced and focus on physical intensity and stimulation, as well as *hot* energy. Depth or sacred sexuality focuses on ecstasy released in the heart as well as the genitals. We may have sought the sacred (love) through the heights of hot physical passion, but that is not necessarily a path to love, though for some women it may be a transitional path. In seeking love, we at times fall into the belief that great chemistry and great sex lead to love (as for some they do); however, they can lead to sharing our bodies, our temples, in a poor bargain—a dance with a demon. Hot sex, although usually temporarily fun and releases repressed or pent-up energy, rarely brings that sense of fulfillment in the form of being seen, accepted, and loved by another and having that expressed physically. Therefore, the temporary fun stirs feelings of both profound sadness and joyful hope.

Although that perspective is a truth, as we engage with the wild woman *more truths are available*, not only this one. From another perspective, all sex, including Mirdad's definition of *hot* or *shallow* sex, can be sacred depending on the lens we look through. In honoring our animal and carnal nature, we may in fact be reverencing the wild woman: Aphrodite or Dionysus, for example. Sex is both sacred and profane. There is an aspect of sex, for instance, that is just sex—i.e., intercourse. And that is okay. Sometimes it is sacred, too. If we try to view it as sacred all the time we fail to see the beauty and value in the ordinary and profane parts of existence and do a disservice to the sacredness of everyday life. An expanded view of sex as both sacred and profane allows for our humanness and is a celebration of embodiment and life. Also, it takes out any unwanted moralism or judgment that may enter and create a negative experience. Having said that, we want to be mindful that we are not harming ourselves by acting out of a place of wounding. To be profane is different from being self-harming.

Mirdad elaborates on *shallow* sex without emotional investment, though keep in mind that it does not serve us to be judgmental of such encounters as shameful. "Behind every shallow sexual interaction, there hides a person who does not want to see or be seen at a deeper level. In such cases, sex is used as a distraction" (2007, pp. 13-14). Many of us value emotional investment in all forms of intimacy, and yet it is scary for many of us. In response to that sentence in Mirdad's book, I offer a dream.

> *I am with a man–woman shape-shifter figure, and we are "escaping." We are on a beach, and a pirate ship, which is not crewed by pirates, is mooring. We dive under the water and hold our breath to go undetected; then we board the ship through a portal that is just large enough for us. We come on board dripping wet into a parlor of wealthy socialites. They notice us but, graciously, do not give us away to the crew— who, even though they are not pirates, would not take well to stowaway escapees. We go to the cabins of the guests and find dresses and other women's clothes. My woman–man friend hides in plain sight by blending in with the rest of the*

guests and boldly proclaims she needs a hairstylist and a manicurist to prepare for the evening. I feel guilty taking clothes from these gracious guests who are not "giving us away"; however, there is also a sense that it is okay to take one dress. I put one on and hide in the closet. Here I am at great risk of being found, for if I am spotted, their reaction will surely be to report me. I realize my risk and decide it is time to come out of the closet and reveal myself as my friend has.

This was not *coming out* in the sense of announcing a change in sexual orientation, which for me would be relatively easy; it is not taboo within myself, or among my family and friends, or even in my comparatively liberal country where same-sex unions have been around as long as I can recall. This coming out of the closet is more vulnerable than that: it means bringing out of the closet my being expressed in embodied sexuality and no longer hiding. When we have to hide our sexuality, it becomes a "skeleton in the closet," and we feel shame. I am dressed beautifully and ready to come out of the closet, to experience letting myself be seen by the other guests on the ship (the vessel, the container of transformation, the body), with supportive guidance from my intrepid, shape-shifting wild woman companion. The dream ended as follows.

I am about to come out; the vessel is back at sea, and we journey now, no longer moored, heading for new, and unknown lands.

So there it is: a new voyage into the unknown is under way.

Re-View

So, what does it mean to be a wild, sexually free woman? It is characterized by a willingness to live with unpredictability, to stay alert, respond to the moment, and act in a way that is true to one's nature. Authentic female sexuality is a mystery that aches to be openly discussed and explored, but not defined or delimited. Embodied presence is essential if women are to find their own forms of sexuality in each moment. Being fully aware in the moment is to be connected to the soul. When experiencing presence during intimacy, we can increase desire and pleasure by anticipating each stroke from the lover. This requires both a well-attuned woman and a safe partner with whom she can feel trust and be vulnerable. Such a situation is not something readily available to some of us—at least not all the time. But ideally, with the right partner(s), we can feel cared for and loved, and that will help us stay present in the moment. It is difficult to sustain focus for extended periods of time regardless of what one is doing—and harder still when the situation asks us to be physically, emotionally, and soulfully naked. Even the so-called goal of being present can be too harsh, and sex can be more relaxed and spontaneous if we are less focused on a goal—even if the goal is presence—and more compassionately accepting of whatever is going on. To stay attuned to our bodies and our partner's, check in and see how *you* feel. It is uncanny how we mirror each other, and the sexual arena is no exception. This does two things: it does invite us back into the present, and it helps us connect with our partner and ourselves. Talking and sharing together are great ways to build intimacy, but we want to avoid becoming too analytical while talking, because we also can talk our way right out of intimacy. Attuning to our body intelligence is a good option for building intimacy and connecting while not talking our way out of Eros's bedchamber.

Many of us want to unite love and sex, but sex without love can be sacred as well. Women (and men) desire intimacy and connection during sexual encounter. Hot sex, too, has its place: it can be fun and orgasmic, and even though it is possible that it can mean *dancing with the demon* and enacting our wounds that are surfacing, it can also be cathartic in transforming those wounds. In pursuing excited heights, we may be trickily hiding ourselves from deep intimacy, and we have to give conscious consideration to what it is we want and then stay attuned to our bodies. Orgasm is not an indication of fulfillment—not for the soul; and even hot sex may not be orgasmic but can still bring sweetness to a woman's life. I hope for all of us at midlife that we can experience the depths and vulnerability of a loving sexuality with another—to come out of the closet—and also that we can experience some of the heights and hotness (and everything in between, as we like).

CHAPTER 6
The Gold

"In Blackwater Woods"

Look, the trees
are turning
their own bodies
into pillars

of light,
are giving off the rich
fragrance of cinnamon
and fulfillment,

the long tapers
of cattails
are bursting and floating away over
the blue shoulders

of the ponds,
and every pond,
no matter what its
name is, is

nameless now.
Every year
everything
I have ever learned

in my lifetime
leads back to this: the fires
and the black river of loss
whose other side

is salvation,
whose meaning
none of us will ever know.
To live in this world

you must be able
to do three things:
to love what is mortal;
to hold it

against your bones knowing
your own life depends on it;
and, when the time comes to let
it go,
to let it go.

Oliver, 1983, p. 82

We began by holding out the question: What are some of the ways a woman who has recovered the wild woman archetype expresses her sexuality and engages in relationships? I set out to write this concluding chapter feeling emboldened that I had learned *something* about the wild woman, women's psychological development, romantic love, and women's sexuality. Then a synchronistic event occurred at that time that deeply dissuaded me. My bear-man told me he made a commitment to a very young woman to be his primary partner in the traditional monogamous model, which was what I had wanted from him. That event triggered my core complexes of feeling unwanted, unworthy of love, not good enough, aging, discarded, and so on. The gift in that painful, humbling disclosure was the reminder that we live with "them"—the "Others." They never fully go away to a state where life becomes suddenly peaceful. The archetypes at the core of the complexes that trigger us are ever present. We just become conscious that they are there, and in doing so, we also become conscious that the unconscious factors are there. We move toward wholeness. We work through the complexes. We breathe slow and deep.

The incident also triggered an imposter complex. I was thinking I had learned something about psychological development and, dare I say, love; but then to be so caught in the talons of an autonomous complex, I suddenly felt as though I had not learned anything. I felt I was an imposter even to attempt to write this chapter summarizing my book—not a very reassuring thought to leave you with. But after a few days, a conversation with him, some dream work, and a few conversations with the wild woman and Aphrodite, finally both the initial insecurity complex that had grabbed me and then the subsidiary imposter complex subsided. Though I was still left with the grief and the loss, they too subsided in time. Time heals a good many things.

We are not alone in the house that we each call *I*, and when the autonomous complexes activate, we are not even master of our own house; *they* are, as the archetypes at the core of the complexes. It is not disempowerment; it is a sharing of our lives with the gods and goddesses or the spirits or whatever names you prefer. The value of the pathologies is that they serve to take us deeper into the realm of the wild woman, the embodied human soul, which is what she yearns for, which is what we yearn for. Hillman and Pozzo (1983) wrote:

> Hard to believe, but the hypochondrias are taking care of us, the depressions are slowing us down, obsessions are ways of polishing the image, paranoid suspicions are ways of trying to see through—all these moves of the patholo- gical are ways we are being loved in the peculiar way the psyche works. (p. 188)

The pathologies and suffering are not going to go away. They are part of what makes us human and, ultimately, vulnerable; and our vulne- rability is beautiful and perfect.

We may engage in human relationships and may enjoy a community of loving relations. By grace, romantic love may find us, and if it does, it *will* include suffering (as well as joy). Suffering through the pains of romantic love is a way into love of soul. Human love is as valuable and sacred as divine love. In fact, they are the same: by engaging in human love (whether romantic, parental, friendly, and so on), we serve the divine; we are engaged in sacred practice when we engage in the intensity of human relatedness. Romantic love, in particular—as most challenging—is a sacred practice through which we can serve soul. Human love and engagement with soul are in- separable. Yes, we can serve soul in creative expression as a means of engagement with the unconscious, but in some ways that approach can be safe because it keeps the struggles and problems of life insulated. This is much like living on a mountaintop, which Jung asserted we cannot do if we wish to individuate; we need the impossible entangle- ments of human relationship to individuate. Human relationship and relationship to soul are not separate but are one and equally valued. *Human love is sacred practice; it is not lesser to "loving God," or loving soul.* Human relationship is *how* we can express our love for the divine—by embracing the gift of our humanness and engaging in the struggles of love and, therefore, individuation.

The remainder of this chapter highlights the discoveries that have seemed most profound, surprising, and unexpected.

The Wild Woman

We danced around defining the wild woman archetype, because how do you define that which is really undefinable? And yet we had to give her form in order to have a relationship to her. There is an interesting phenomenon in that it is she who gives us the imaginings that make it possible for us to personify her as an autonomous entity separate from what we primarily know as ourselves. She, who is the image maker, is the one we have been tracking. She has provided us with myriad images and imaginings of herself. We are challenged to define her and allow for her differentiated forms to be related to separately. It is a big challenge: she shows up in so many different forms. In *real* life:

> *It is early March; dwarf irises stretched out their purple fingers yesterday, the snow piles shrank, and the groggy black bear hunkered down in my yard to tear into garbage that a neighbor had carelessly disposed of. It is early for her to be stirring, and I was delighted she found her way to my yard again this year. Knowing she resides here, we human locals are normally careful about garbage and other bear attractants in order to keep her wild. Staying wild is what ensures she stays alive. If she gets too domesticated by our presence and an easy food supply, she will be captured and relocated or, possibly, shot. Most years, this adjustment to living with an awakened bear goes smoothly, and we human animals adapt quickly to coexist responsibly with her. I wonder whether she has cubs again this year.*

Here we have her bear form, awake from her winter slumber in her "other reality" of the dream time. Now she roams, looking for food, wild, somewhat unpredictable, and hungry, but still slow. She will find her way to the river, where the pink salmon are running, and she will feast alongside the bald eagle and the raven. It is an abundant ecosystem here, and she must be allowed to follow her instincts to find her way to sustenance, undistracted by garbage that is easy—and possibly lethal. We must take the cue and let the wild woman roam in the wilderness of the psyche.

The wild woman has presented herself in other equally potent guises throughout this book as well: shape-shifter, moon goddess, and the hermaphroditic woman with the phallus, along with more-familiar terms like anima–animus, Psyche, psyche, and soul. I have often used the terms interchangeably, but that is not quite right, because they differ to varying degrees. However, a funny paradox occurred: the figures seemed to become more differentiated and as though all of them were aspects of a single figure in different dress. That paradox of many and one is fitting for the wild woman, because she does have many forms, and each form is different. I invited the figures to a transference dialogue in order to deepen my relationship with each of them.

I imagined a discussion around a fire where we all gathered. My intention was to discern the differences more clearly. In addition to me (the ego, consciousness, or *I*), the others were the wild woman as Psyche, as a personification of the psyche; the moon goddess who had impregnated me in the earlier dream; the shape-shifter who initially showed up in the forest fire dream; the woman lover with the fabulous phallus; bear; and my male partner as a personification of an aspect of the animus. It was a light, playful encounter, like an informal meeting. I include a bit of it here.

> *Me: Thank you for coming. It is an honor to have you all together.*
> *Wild Woman: —and separate. (laughter)*
> *Me: That is why I have invited you; to distinguish you better, to understand you as more separate.*

Animus: Well, I'm separate. Well, not from Bear.
Bear: Yes. I'm separate, except for Animus. Well, and Shape-shifter,
and Wild Woman.
Shape-shifter: I'm separate and everyone at the same time.
Moon Goddess: Well, I am not Animus, except in his Bear form.
Wild Woman: We are separate and not separate. We are like this.
(draws overlapping circles that make a single circle) We overlap into
one another. (The symbol she drew was a mandala—a Self-
symbol—that looked like a flower or a kaleidoscope image.)

The dialogue continued for several pages. I discovered that the moon
goddess is different from the hermaphrodite lover, for example, because
the lover is more able to bridge the personal, and the goddess is more
impersonal. I asked why the male Animus figure was there in the
personification of my partner. "Because Psyche follows love," said Wild
Woman. He therefore serves as a guide, though often as a somewhat
"hapless dumbling," not intentionally acting as a guide. "Isn't it always
love that calls us to our greatest adventures and potential? That is why
it is here in this form."

Wild Woman differentiated herself from Psyche (as a personification of the psyche): "We are not quite the same, no. Sometimes. I am
embodied always. I'm rarely on Olympus. But I too follow love—sometimes." This was quite typical of the slippery nature of the entire
dialogue. It was fluid and tricky to arrive at succinct clarity, but that
itself was a form of clarity; such is the nature of these figures in the
psyche. In the myth, Psyche wedded on Olympus can be read as
symbolic of the human soul's regression into the realm of the gods and
goddesses and therefore into the unconscious—further from personal
experience and further from embodied human experience. The whole
dialogue was valuable, but in particular it offered an understanding of
the together-but-separate overlapping nature of these figures, which
combined to make a single Self symbol—both a monotheistic image
and a pluralistic image.

Ultimately, the wild woman is an archetype; she is what makes women women. She is the archetype of the animal woman. Just as the acorn is the seed of the oak and, if it grows, will always produce an oak and not a pine, the wild woman is the archetype of a woman and will always produce a woman. I initially mused that she could also exist in men as the feminine aspect; I no longer think that is the case, though the anima can—at least for this book's imagining.

This entire book has been vulnerably personal (much more than I intended, hoped, or imagined it would be) and representative of my experience with these figures. Just as each oak is different from all other oaks, each woman is different from all other women; and therefore, how these figures show up for each woman will be unique to her. That has been my experience, and in the bigger picture, it has been an essential piece of my particular process of individuation. I hope this book connects to a deeper meaningfulness that resonates for other wild women.

I wanted to know who a woman was before she was "made" by her culture. We wrestled with the question, and we continued on to its partner questions: How can a woman live in the culture and not be caged by it? And, the more she is related to her own wild womanliness, what forms do her romantic or sexual relationships or both take? Those questions may be unanswerable. The questions themselves are what matters: the questions create the path. Just as we have to hold the tensions and lean into the uncomfortable emotions, we have to lean into the questions. It is the seeking that matters; in seeking the answers, we find our way forward and we outgrow, integrate, or transform our painful challenges. Surfers search the world for the perfect wave, which is a metaphor for life; it is the search that creates the journey and gives purpose and meaning to life. In searching for answers to the questions regarding the wild woman, we become propelled on to the next and then the next step of our stroll through the wilds of our lives. Bud Harris (2007), a Jungian analyst, cites Catholic monk and author Thomas Merton, on this idea of living into the questions.

Mystics and Jungians agree on a basic point: we cannot try to resolve the tension of life by disowning its unpleasant aspects and attempting to live perpetually in a bright, pleasant, protected realm—especially one fenced in by safe questions and endless rules about right and wrong. If we hold the world at a distance we are simply "clinging to one horn," as Merton would say. And we will have lost our life, for we will have cut ourselves off from the places where the Divine and the world interact to form turning points of transformation. Living into the contradictions is knowing the questions in their deepest sense and thereby to live into the answers. The "peace that passes understanding," for example, comes from fully accepting the tumultuous and transformative nature of life as it moves us deeper into wholeness. (p. 87)

The questions can show us the struggles, such as: How can I love someone and move on, knowing he has made a choice that is incompatible for my feeling life and my values? The struggle to find our way is what shapes the path. The answer is simply to respond to each moment as it presents.

Another question we explored is: How is a woman to live in the culture and not be captive to it? There is an inherent tension in the question, a tension that has been present throughout this book, as manifest, for example, in the fantasy to move to Nicaragua and become a surf yogini. The tension comes from the poles of wanting freedom from culture but realizing we are *in* the culture. We are, in fact, part of culture. We are also wild, independent, and autonomous women— women who, as each petal opens, come to know our own morality, ethics, and rules to live by. In each moment, we can thrive in the tensions and respond from our instinctive and intuitive wisdom—our embodied, wild animal woman sense. We become related to our animality, with all of our good instincts, which reliably guide us in each wild and precious moment.

Trusting our innate womanly wisdom, we can live more deeply into the contradictions and no longer need so-called understanding or clarity. Of course those things are nice, but instead, we can move toward a greater sense of wholeness and blossom into more-profound persons. The oft-used metaphor of wine comes to mind: we say that the more complex a wine is with subtleties and depth, the more it has character and, therefore, the more it is rich and delicious. Women are truly like wine: we improve as we age, as we build complexity and character, and as we acquire the ability to live more deeply into the questions (as though, with an intoxicating grin Dionysus appropriately makes his presence known in that metaphor).

There is value in living into the paradoxes and tensions. As contradictions, or paradoxes, are "lived into," our perception of them is transformed. Paradoxes only *seem* self-contradictory. But on deeper investigation, they are transformational and are actually also true. As our personality opens to truths and experiences larger than we could have previously comprehended, the Self creates within us a more profound personality. This is the process of individuation. The more we can open ourselves to the seemingly impossible contradictions, the more we open ourselves to the psyche, which is an immeasurably creative force extremely capable of presenting solutions that are far beyond what we are able to initially grasp. We come to know that there is nothing to figure out and that there is no path, but that that *is* the path. The path is the psychic wilderness.

Gary Snyder (1990) told a story to talk about that path as well.

During one of the long meditation retreats called *sesshin* the *rōshi* [teacher] lectured on the phrase "the perfect way is without difficulty. Strive hard!" This is the fundamental paradox of the way. One can be called on not to spare one's very bones in the intensity of effort, but at the same time we must be reminded that the path itself offers no hindrance, and there is a suggestion that the effort itself can lead one astray. . . . "A path that can be followed is not a *spiritual* path." The actuality of things cannot be confined within so linear an image as a road. . . . The way is without difficulty—it does not itself propose obstacles to us, it is open in all directions. We do, however, get in our own way—so the Old Teacher said "Strive hard!" (pp. 160-161)

What we are striving hard to do is to get out of our own way, and because we all have our own ways of being in our own way, the path will be different for everyone. The areas of relationships and sexuality are where I strive to find ease and grace, as many women do; it is the most common theme in my clinical practice. Part of the paradox, however, is that it is the striving to untangle the knots that enriches soul. If I ever do "get" relationships, it will be because I have finally stopped trying and can just let them happen and be. But maybe that is not meant to be my path. The search for love has filled my life with meaningful experiences and has brought the honey and sweetness as well as the sting and the ache. A friend once said to me: "Why do you try so hard? Love just happens or it doesn't." I understand the wisdom in that simplicity, but wisdom is also gained in engaging with the beautiful mystery. That is how the questions and the questing have guided my path. The path is the razor's edge created by the tensions. The razor's edge is no less than holding the tension of the opposites and not opting for one side or the other, until that unconscious material can make itself known to consciousness. This applies to being in this culture yet not confined by it, so that it does not stifle our ability to individuate. Individuation entails being part of this culture. It's not something outside of us that is trying to confine us. So, maybe the question is: how do we participate in culture without being confined by our own selves? Throughout this book, I have written about culture as it is often referred to, like it is something *out there* some other thing that acts upon us but is not us; however, all of us are culture. We are acting upon our own selves. We too are like the circles overlapping to make one circle—and in this case, that circle is culture. We can affect how we do that by how we relate to ourselves and how we relate to others. The expression the Lakota use in recognition of others is *all my relations*, an understanding that extends beyond living and ancestral family to all humanity, animals, plants, and minerals—the entire natural world and beyond. All of us are related.

After returning from a fabulous vacation with my son, I was replenishing our cupboards by making purchases at the local grocery store at midday on a Tuesday. A situation was erupting outside between three men in the parking lot while I was inside paying. A woman and her child came rushing in and asked the checker to call security. A bony woman in her late 50s turned out to be the security who came to assist. Through the door, I saw two of the men beating the third man, and I suggested to the checker that she call 9-1-1 as well. She did not. I always carry my phone, but that time, for some odd reason, I did not have it. As the situation unfolded, the two men violently pinned the third man to the ground, one kneeling on his chest and ribs with his full body weight, the other yanking his hips trying to flip him over. The pinned man was motionless, no longer resisting or struggling, and yet the two men continued to assault him. By that point, still in the store, I had heard he had apparently stolen food. People were saying things like, "He was a bad man, and that's what happens to bad men." A swarm mentality was erupting, and still no one I could see had yet called 9-1-1. I considered buying his stolen groceries for him, but that moment was long past. Then I asked two other people for phones, to no avail. I was very upset and did not know what to do to remedy the situation; it felt too dangerous to engage directly, because the men pinning him down were clearly possessed by something volatile and Ares-like in their vigilant righteousness. I decided to get myself home and then call 9-1-1. As I was leaving, two police cars screeched in, almost hitting my car. I was so thankful to see them; the situation called for an objective third party with authority. (Normally, being a bit of a rebel, I do not welcome such authority.) I got home and cried; it hurt to have witnessed such violence. Where was compassion? I recognized all my relations in that episode. Yes, in the man seeking food who was violently assaulted, but also in the two men who became gripped by such a rageful archetype. (Their violence seemed so much worse than called for by the theft of some food.) There were also my relations who supported the violence by either apathy or actual encouragement. Someone else called the police—I just did not see who—and that person is yet another relation. Then too, the police; I do not know how the situation concluded, but I imagined they would resolve it with some clear objectivity.

Four nights prior to that day, I had had a dream.

The police arrested a teenage boy who was living in my suite and dealing drugs, unbeknownst to me. The boy was being threatened by drug lords and was in danger and therefore endangering my son and me. By arresting the boy, the police took the threat out of my house, thereby keeping him and my son and me safe—and I did not even know it was happening. I learned later that they had been surveilling my house for 10 months.

Dream and material reality intersect here, and I have to welcome an intervention by a third authority that belongs to culture: the police. We are culture, and all of these are my relations, inside and out.

Perfection versus Wholeness

What is this wholeness that Jungians talk about, of which the Self is the ordering principle? How is wholeness different from perfection? We cannot talk about wholeness without also talking about in-dividuation, "the process by which a person becomes a psychological 'in-dividual,' that is, a separate, indivisible unity or 'whole'" (Storr, 1983, p. 212). Becoming a whole individual means we are held together by the Self, which is the mediating archetype of both the conscious and unconscious. We cannot be conscious of the unconscious factors, but we can be conscious that the unconscious factors have *at least* as much sway over our lives as our ego consciousness does—and probably much more. Wholeness and totality occur in a well-developed personality in which the ego is conscious of the unconscious in the psyche as a codetermining factor in one's life. One is mature enough to develop as an individual—separate from the collective—and recognize that one is more than one's own ego consciousness. Storr elaborated:

> The self, of which the mandala is a symbol, is the archetype of unity and totality. . . . Jung believed that only exceptional individuals reached the peaks of individual development. Individuation means parting company with the crowd; and this at first accentuates loneliness, and may seem alarming. Most human beings are content to remain safely with the majority. (p. 20)

It is a painfully lonely path, and it fuels the longing for romantic relationship, which has been the catalyst for the journey. It all fits together.

The quest for wholeness involves taking into account all of those neglected parts of one's personality: for example, one may be predominantly intuitive and have to develop her sensation function in order to develop an awareness of areas that were pushed away into shadow. Jung wrote (*CW 9i*, paras. 489-524), "The whole must necessarily include not only consciousness but the illimitable field of unconscious occurrences as well, and . . . the ego can be no more than the centre of the field of consciousness" (in Storr, 1983, p. 213). Although the ego has dominion over consciousness, Jung did not believe there was a center that was the ego equivalent and had dominion over the unconscious. On the contrary, he found it unlikely because of the chaotic nature and "unsystematic form" that the unconscious phenomena manifest. Here we can suggest that all of the archetypes vie for their positions, whereas the poor ego center can feel quite bandied about. The Self, Jung suggested, was the center point between the conscious and unconscious.

Perfection, on the other hand, really has very little to do with wholeness and is actually antithetical to it. One cannot be whole if one is striving for perfection. Perfection is only one pole—the bright, shiny, everything-is-wonderful pole. Imperfection—in fact, all of the painful, icky inferiorities that trigger our complexes and are the things we tend to want to reject about ourselves—is required for wholeness. Wholeness includes *all* of who we are. It is everything that makes us fabulous wonderful women who have everything we consider pathologies: jealousy, neediness, insecurity, and the like. If we are to engage with the wild woman, it is necessary that we get over our pursuit of perfection and our desire to transcend all of the painful emotions, pathologies, and suffering and instead engage with our earthy humanness. It is interesting to follow the etymology: *humus* (composted soil, earth, ground) is the Latin root of the words *human, humble, humility,* and *humor.* It reminds us of our origins: ashes to ashes and dust to dust. We are not gods and goddesses, but we are the vessels they can be seen in as they live through us. In his poem "The Guest House," Rumi captured what it means not to be alone in one's own house:

> This being human is a guest house.
> Every morning a new arrival.
> A joy, a depression, a meanness,
> some momentary awareness comes
> as an unexpected visitor.
> Welcome and entertain them all!. . . .
> Be grateful for whatever comes,
> because each has been sent
> as a guide from beyond.
>
> Trans. 2001, p. 109

This is poetry of individuation—coming to know all those who arrive at our house and how we would do well to treat each as a noble guest. As gracious hosts, we are guided toward wholeness.

Show Up and Surrender

Let us explore the concepts of showing up and surrendering because most of us like to be in control; it is comfortable. By *showing up*, I mean finding the discipline and the will to be present for what is soulful and meaningful—despite all the mind chatter that talks us out of it. The ego can get very afraid when it has to show up for something it has to surrender control to. Examples are plentiful, but a few include researching and writing, any creative artistic venture, a shamanic ceremony, perching on your meditation seat, or engaging in a relationship. When the ego is no longer the one driving, it can become incredibly wily in presenting all manner of rational, logical, right-seeming reasons not to participate, not to show up. For example, my home is never more polished then when I am engaged in a writing project. "Oh, I'll just clean the bathroom before I sit down to the computer." All manner of distractions can be more appealing to the ego than giving over to the creative process.

The ego is smart. So, how do you outfox a fox? Sometimes listening to the ego's reservations, fears, rational concerns, and, occasionally, childish tantrums helps. Say thank you to the ego for its warnings and intention to provide safety and protection. And rally your courage. We need a strong ego that can access the will and the courage to show up anyway; the ego must be disciplined enough to both show up and then surrender control. *Discipline* has its roots in *disciple*, which has Latin origins in a word meaning *learn, pupil, student*. We want to learn what we need for our own individuation. We must commit ourselves to ourselves. We want to hear the concerns and then still show up for our learning, even though it means the conscious personality is not the one in control; if it were, we would hardly be learning anything new, because we would already be conscious of it. So, after we muster our courage, the next step is the terrifying inevitability of surrendering ego control so that we can learn what we do not yet know.

Jung wrote about our need to humbly recognize our humanness and surrender our ego's desire for control.

> Western man has no need of more superiority over nature, whether outside or inside. He has both in almost devilish perfection. What he lacks is conscious recognition of his inferiority to the nature around and within him. He must learn that he may not do exactly as he wills. If he does not learn this, his own nature will destroy him. (Jung, 1958/2010, p. 356 [CW 11, para. 535])

Much of our culture has become too one-sided as we mistakenly try to control our lives and our world. We do not have dominion over nature, whether outside or inside. In talking about trying to be superior over nature, it is appropriate (and convenient for this writing) that Jung uses the term *devilish perfection*: the quest for perfection is devilish because it will destroy us. Accepting our failings and weaknesses and vulnerabilities takes strength. The less we try to control and reign, the more resilient and enriched we become as we access the wholeness available to us as undividable individual personalities. Further, to challenge the semantics, *we are perfect* just as we are, with our inferiorities and shameful secrets that we try to hide and reject. We may not be flawless, but we are perfectly imperfect. Try looking yourself in the eye in the mirror and saying, "I am perfect," and feel yourself accept all of who you are. It can be tough for many of us, even harder than saying, "I love you," to yourself.

At the end of drafting this book, I had an opportunity to go to Costa Rica on a twelve-day, yoga-surf trip with a small group. One can imagine my delight at the timeliness, and twelve days offered a good middle way compared with fully relocating to Central America. I am predominantly introverted and had been feeling the urge to be in community more, so the prospect of traveling in an intimate-sized group was appealing. Another awareness was a felt presence in our circle of six surfing yogis, because we were essentially all strangers to one another but discovered numerous links and commonalities. The trip itself took on its own life as the schedule adapted to meet the needs of the collective. It was as though we had become part of a living entity that was held together by something profoundly other. Sometimes it is easy to surrender to the archetypal other, as it was in this case, but at other times it is difficult. Even with something we enjoy, such as writing or relationships, we can talk ourselves out of showing up to the meeting of the archetypal other because we cannot know the outcome; entering the unknown feels perilous.

Further, even something we enjoy can become complicated by multiple archetypal presences so that we experience conflicting pulls. At that point, we can feel torn asunder as we experience a plurality of truths and not one clear and simple truth. The ideas of "finding your truth" and "your true self" and so on trouble me a great deal, because so often, more than one archetypal presence is having a say. There is no resolution with Aphrodite, Hera, and Artemis in one psyche; all three have different modes of expression. Further, we have little say about who does what or when. This is where living moment to moment with the instincts of the wild women is helpful: we can differentiate who is visiting in that moment and then decide how we will respond. All we really have any control over is our response.

Projection

An aspect of this book that had greater significance than I had expected is the phenomenon of projection. Thus far, this book has focused on erotic projection, but as a way to get deeper into that phenomenon, let us explore a more expansive definition too. Von Franz (1995) wrote extensively and in depth on the topic, picking up from Jung, who adopted the term from Freud, although Jung's definition, because his view of the unconscious differed from Freud's, gave the concept a new interpretation. Essentially, both Jung and von Franz agree that projection is used to

> describe a psychological fact that can be observed every-
> where in the everyday life of human beings, namely, that
> in our ideas about other people and situations we are often

liable to make misjudgments that we later have to correct, having acquired better insight. (von Franz, 1995, pp. 1-2)

Accordingly, we are always in a state of projection, and it is not confined to erotic projection. It arises from the unconscious and carries on until there is a disturbance. For example, for a week now, a robin has flown into my window repeatedly from sunrise to sunset. I have tried to deter it by hanging objects in the window and eliminating reflection (which is already interesting symbolic language), but the bird persists in flying into my window. I have projected onto this robin, after a week, that it is a stupid bird that keeps banging its head in its attempts to try to mate. I identify with this stupid bird that keeps doing the same thing over and over, even though all it gets is a headache and not a mate. I can reflect where I do that in my own life: where I keep flying into my own reflection, which simply is not working. Today I cleaned up the week-long accumulation of bird waste, which gathered some frustrated anger, so I told the bird that if it kept persisting, I would shoot at it with my water bottle. That wouldn't be good for either of us. We are working things out. It is a symbolic message inspired from nature. Nature is such a clear mirror for projection work because it is untainted by another human's humanness. I have projected my own reflection onto the robin. It is not I, nor I it, though we are probably doing the same thing to some degree: trying to mate with our own reflection and wondering why it is so indifferent to us; because it is a reflection of ourselves, we are not engaged with an actual other. The whole experience is projection—I project onto the bird in this case. It is helpful to contemplate how I project myself onto men and how they must not feel seen, and so they reflect back to me indifference. After all, who wants to be with someone who is not seeing them? I can begin to differentiate the man I am projecting onto from the projected thought by getting curious about who he is and what he stands for.

What we can understand as we remove projections is the image of the unconscious psychic contents which were projected onto the object and which are breaking into our consciousness so that we may now be able to integrate them. This is a process that never gets fully achieved because we are always moving into other states of projection. Perluss wrote on the phenomenon even further.

> We can certainly do our best to make our projections as conscious as possible, but as von Franz reminds us, it is not a "projection" per se until recognized as such; until it causes us some trouble usually. In other words, we are in a state of unconscious participation all the time but are just not aware of this. This is just the way we relate to others and the world. (B. Perluss, personal communication, 2014)

Projection is how we see ourselves in the world, but if we get too caught in the process of self-reflection—as this robin is teaching us—it keeps us out of life. We can become too self-absorbed. At some point, we have to stop looking at ourselves and just live our lives; otherwise, we risk missing it. This, of course, is not a regression back into unconsciousness; though, it is a way of hiding.

The next piece amounts to the question: Who is dreaming whom? Are we dreaming—projecting—our reality. Or is Psyche dreaming us and creating her reality? It is both: life is created in the space between subject and object, self and other, self and psyche, and the interchange between us and Other. This interchange is ultimately what creates reality, whether conscious or unconscious. How we respond to what we are presented with is what creates life and all varieties of reality. The archetypes of the psyche collude to collide with compatible patterning that we think is personal but that really belongs to the unconscious. Psyche—and the plethora of archetypes contained within—dreams the world into reality, and we are but a part of her dream. As von Franz said, "We can say that even the Self can become aware of itself only with the help of the ego, only in ego-consciousness, which is the mirror" (1995, p. 188). I no longer believe that the gods and goddesses personifying the core of the complexes are ambivalent to us—they mirror back our personal relationships to them. If we have a negative mother relationship, that is what is mirrored back. If we have a protective, nurturing mother relationship, that is what is mirrored back. If we believe we are fundamentally alone, that is what is mirrored back. If we believe the gods and goddesses love us, that is what is mirrored back. And so on. As we relate to them, the relationships transform, and so do we.

Von Franz wrote more about this Self-mirroring that occurs through ego consciousness as the mirror of the Self when she examined the dream that Jung reported in *Memories, Dreams, Reflections* (1961). In the dream, Jung comes to a small chapel and enters to find a beautiful flower arrangement on the altar and a yogi seated in front of it in the lotus position in deep meditation. On closer look, he sees that the yogi had his face. "I started in profound fright, and awoke with the thought: 'aha, so he is the one who is meditating me. He has a dream, and I am it.' I knew that when he awakened, I would no longer be" (von Franz, 1995, p. 158). The dream is fabulously simple and profound in this regard: the Self personified as the yogi dreams itself into the ego and thereby into the material world. Reflecting on Jung's dream, it opened up my fantasy of being a surf yogini in a new way. It prompted me to examine it as a purely symbolic image: the yogi as a Self symbol as in Jung's dream while riding the waves of the ocean as a symbol of riding the energy of the unconscious (the ocean)—in particular, the emotional waves on the surface—and not being crushed and overwhelmed by the strong affect (caused by the archetypes) but transferring that raw force into kinetic energy. Fantasies, like dreams, have many layers of meanings.

The drive toward individuation is innate and directed by a force greater than the ego. Relationship (whether or not romantic) is required for individuation, precisely because we start with projection; and through reflection, we self-actualize and learn about ourselves on our path toward wholeness. All romantic relationships in time will reveal what is projection or not. How we respond to this newfound material we call projection is what matters. Do you leave the relationship— which might be the right thing to do—or stick with it and work it out?

Once we have done much work to remove projections, a different kind of relationship can develop and we may have the opportunity to choose whether we want to continue to be in relationship to that person or not. If not, we may meet someone else and have the opportunity to engage in the process of removing projections from the new person. Von Franz recognizes that once projections are withdrawn,

> this in no way annuls or sets aside the relationship. On the contrary, a genuine, "deeper" relation emerges, no longer rooted in egotistical moods, struggles, or illusions but rather in the feeling of being connected to one another via an absolute, objective principle. (1995, p. 174)

If we are introspective, we are probably at least somewhat conscious of our own unconscious projections, but that can create the problem of being too analytical in relationship, which is damaging to intimacy and is also a way to hide from emotional vulnerability. The counterbalance to being too cerebral is to be more animal and instinctive, more embodied and wild as women.

Relationship and Sexuality

If I am nakedly honest, I engaged in this topic to try to come to terms with the relationship struggle I was engaged in. Maybe that is obvious to the reader, but it was not obvious to me initially. It is embarrassing even to write that, because who in her right mind would make such an investment of time, psychological energy, and money? Well, a woman who was struggling deeply to come to terms with herself would—a woman who was fully in the throes of individuation through the torments of love. Even though I love the man I refer to as my partner and even though seeking mutual love (as *I* wanted it to be expressed) has been the catalyst for opening up to complexities that I could never have otherwise imagined, it is—and it is not—all that much about *him*. It has been about the journey toward myself.

There is a deepening of our understanding of the imaging of two kinds of significant love relationships that Hollis (1998) and Johnson (1983) and other Jungians have examined: love of soul and human love. Both require relationships, and even though they are two separate relationships, human love often nourishes the soul, and soul love can in turn nourish human love. The irony, of course, is that the yearning takes us into deeper relationship with the wild woman and hence the soul, which was probably the deeper yearning all along. A human love relationship may never actually manifest the way we desire; nothing we do can control that because only the other can—the other who resides as an autonomous entity in the psyche. So, if we surrendered to her, we would find that we could come to love our suffering too, knowing it bears us down into the fertile soil of soul and knowing we are fully engaged in our one wild and precious life.

As we come to the end of this book, I have surprisingly little to say about sexuality. What started as *the* most difficult problem is now simply not much of a problem at all. I do not have any solutions, because I find I have no further concerns with sexuality at present. It seems I have overvalued it for much of my adult life, and now it "just is." That feels easy and welcome. There is a stillness in my being that feels unconcerned with the whole matter of sexual relationship. It seems this was an area on which I had placed too much importance— probably because of the circumstances of my wounding. There is a relief that that difficulty is gone (at least for now) and a calm curiosity about what will follow in time.

Much of the fantasy of sexual union involves both the pursuit of spiritual heights and the symbolic desire for the *coniunctionis*, the uniting of the opposites. Through this book, the problem of liberating my psyche from the unconscious forces was clarified; I was trying to be free of so-called cultural forces, but that was only partly true. In understanding this as a greater psychological and spiritual process, we become more conscious of the unconscious. We are not the master of our house; rather, we cohabit with gods and goddesses, including the wild woman, with her embodied and instinctual way of knowing. In recognizing that we are the ones being dreamed, a *coniunctionis* occurred—not out of my effort and, yet, *also* out of my effort. It is not "done"—the journey does not end, possibly not even at death; rather, a core complex or, probably, several complexes were related to with consciousness and through symbolic engagement, through this process. Through that psychological union, the yearning for sexual relationship has changed. My approach to and attitude toward romantic love are fundamentally different. The once very large and confusing problems of relationships and sexuality are no longer so large. We can value human relationship as a way to further enrich personality and fully engage in life—even if "endings" initially appear unhappy.

In conclusion, this whole project turned out to be essentially a spiritual path or, rather, a soul path. It is a path that embraces and celebrates our humanness and is not seeking to transcend to spiritual heights or escape the confines of the matter of the body. Rather, it is a way to live in this world and celebrate each glorious moment with its monotony, pain, joy, and pleasure. It is essential to recognize that the unconscious is a codetermining factor along with consciousness and that, with conscious will alone, it is futile to attempt to force or control anything. The qualities of receptivity, patience, and acceptance all make the transition from one conscious attitude to another smoother as we practice action through nonaction, or *wu wei*. In other words, quit trying to force anything—especially something as archetypal as love. Instead, allow the yearning to guide our journey. Interestingly, the yearning has subsided completely I have enjoyed a prolonged state of contentedness.

Jung uses the expression, "It is not I who lives, it lives me" (in Wilhelm, 1931, p. 131). That summarizes the journey this book took me on. It began with a search for romantic love but has taken me to the understanding that the one I thought I was tracking—the wild woman—was actually tracking me, with a whole entourage.

Afterword

Some years have passed since the first words of this book were drafted for my doctoral dissertation research; therefore, I want to add an update on yearning—or lack thereof—for a relationship. I find my musings now are around the idea of: Why would I want to partner and give up the freedom that singleness has to offer? There are so many types of relationships to help us grow. There are so many places to channel our libido or creative energy. I find much of mine goes into writing, my clinical therapy practice, my time with my son, my relationships with my friends, and my two dogs. I feel present to my life which is rich and full. Life feels complete. As I tend to have many creative endeavors on the go, it is overwhelming at times, but I have moved into a place of loving my life and wondering: why would I change that? Romantic love has not alighted. I would still welcome it as a blessing if it did, but I am not yearning nor looking, instead I am grateful for the ease and generativity I am experiencing at this new stage of life. I wish peace and ease for all women, whether they partner or not, and hope they too find gratitude and meaning on the other side of their struggles. I wish all women and men soulful lives.

I also want to say more about the deeply personal and transformative nature of my research methodology since it is not traditional. Alchemical hermeneutics is a qualitative research method. The approaches used in the natural sciences are quantitative and are not appropriate for this study of human psychology. As Deborah Tolman and Mary Brydon-Miller (2001) write: "Lived experience is, for Dilthey, the primary, first-order category that captures an individual's immediate, concrete 'experience as such.' It is, in other words, an act of consciousness itself; it is something that is lived in and lived through" (p. 47). That approach to research gives value to the lived experience, including reading the text of lived relationships for the purpose of grounding the work in praxis. Romanyshyn (2007) credits the valuable contribution Dilthey made in the late nineteenth century; however, he wrote, "Jung's elaboration of the psychoid archetype exposes three problems with it" (p. 239): "Dilthey leaves no room for a science of soul; psychology . . . must be pluralistic in its methods and interdisciplinary in its character; [and] . . . the unconscious [is left] out of the picture in the human sciences" (pp. 239-240). The method of alchemical hermeneutics is corrective to those shortcomings and makes room for the soul, the unconscious, and is pluralistic; therefore it is particularly well suited for this depth psychology qualitative research book.

In addition to depth psychology, I approach this book through the lens of social constructionism, which focuses on uncovering the ways people participate in the construction of their perceived social realities. It involves looking at the ways social phenomena get created, institutionalized, known, and made into tradition by humans. This is relevant because the expression of the wild woman archetype gets socialized out of women from birth. One example is the role of wife, which, in its dominant enactment, is no longer relevant and in service to women who have reclaimed the wild woman archetype. The role in its current form is not innate but is a social construct that has become largely outmoded and needs updating and reimagining, or other options should become more dominant so that there is an expanded view of relationship roles.

As researchers and writers, we are called to our topics through our wounds and complexes, and the transference relationship between the researcher and the work is alchemical and transformative. The transformation acts on the researcher as well as on the work, but it is also never complete; the process of transformation is dynamic and ongoing. As the researcher, my task for this book was to show up and then surrender to it, acknowledging that it is its own entity. The field of depth psychology—as a tradition in service to the autonomous psyche—also individuates as we are in relationship to the unconscious; this is a belief many depth psychotherapists hold, beginning with Jung

(1958/2010). The transference field works largely at the level of the unconscious, though we can consciously hold space for that alchemical process. At least four levels are affected: the researcher, the topic, the field of depth psychology, and the autonomous psyche. For each, it is an ongoing process that expands by being contributed to.

This research invites a hermeneutic spiral rather than a hermeneutic circle, which opens the dialogue between the researcher and the work on conscious and unconscious levels by including dreams, synchronicities, and active imaginations. The unconscious then has its place in whatever way it presents. Romanyshyn (2007) describes various techniques—in particular, transference dialogues—that are like the active imaginations developed by Jung. Transference dialogues are ways of "letting go of the work," which "refers to the researcher's conscious relation to the work . . . letting go, the researcher surrenders his or her outlines so that he or she can be addressed by the threads that tie him or her more subtly to the work" (p. 140). Romanyshyn suggests creating a situation that invites the unconscious and offers guidelines on how that can be done. In this way, the others in the research, particularly the ancestral, can have a voice; the work does not belong to the researcher but is differentiated as its own entity. Simultaneously, "there is no separation between the work and the person doing the work, the person who, in working on the topic, is also being worked on, and even at times worked over, by the topic" (p. 269). Appropriately, there is a paradox of *differentiation* and *no separation*. In alchemy, the first phase of the transformation is one of separation and differentiation through expanding consciousness. Once differentiation occurs and consciousness is brought in, there can be a reunification or *coniunctionis* but not a return to the original state; consciousness must be maintained.

Hermeneutics has traditionally used text for interpretation, but it is now widely recognized that almost anything can be seen as a text. In "How Is Psychology a Mythology?" Paris (2008) wrote about Jacques Derrida's expanded notion of text to "consider the unconscious as a text and analysis as a deconstruction of that same text. . . . Text, in his personal dictionary, is everything and anything that can be interpreted or deconstructed" (p. 220). This book includes relationships, dreams, synchronicities, and active imaginations (transference dialogues) as symbolic texts. Reading data from those texts made it possible to describe and interpret the experience in order to create meaningfulness and to honor soul as a perspective. Ultimately, this book serves the soul.

References

Apuleius. (1998). *The golden ass.* New York, NY: Penguin.

Avens, R. (1984). *The new gnosis: Heidegger, Hillman and angels.* Woodstock, CT: Spring.

Berry, P. (2001). The rape of Demeter/Persephone and neurosis. In C. Downing (Ed.), *The long journey home* (pp. 197-205). Boston, MA: Shambhala.

Bolen, J. S. (1984). *Goddesses in everywoman: Powerful archetypes in women's lives.* New York, NY: Harper Perennial.

Bonheim, J. (1997). *Aphrodite's daughters: Women's sexual stories and the journey of the soul.* New York, NY: Fireside.

Cagen, S. (2004). *Quirkyalone: A manifesto for uncompromising romantics.* New York, NY: HarperCollins.

Cambray, J. (2009). *Synchronicity: Nature and psyche in an inter-connected universe.* College Station, TX: A&M University Press.

Carotenuto, A. (1989). *Eros and pathos: Shades of love and suffering.* Toronto, Canada: Inner City Books.

Castillejo, I. C. (1973). *Knowing woman: A feminine psychology.* Boston, MA: Shambhala.

Chödrön, P. (2000). *When things fall apart.* Boston, MA: Shambhala.

Corbett, L. (2012a). *The biblical story of Job and Jung's answer to Job* (audio podcast). Retrieved from Pacifica Graduate Institute Course DJA 850 DesireToLearn site.

Corbett, L. (2012b). *Overview of Jung's approach to spirituality and religion* (audio podcast). Retrieved from Pacifica Graduate Institute course DJA 850 DesireToLearn site.

de Beauvoir, S. (1949). *The second sex.* New York, NY: Random House.

Diamond, L. M. (2008). *Sexual fluidity: Understanding women's love and desire.* London, England: Harvard University Press.

Douglas, C. (1990). *The woman in the mirror: Analytical psychology and the feminine.* Lincoln, NE: iUniverse.

Downing, C. (1981). *The goddess: Mythological images of the feminine.* Lincoln, NE: iUniverse.

Downing, C. (1989). *Myths and mysteries of same-sex love.* New York, NY: Continuum.

215

Downing, C. (1990). *Psyche's sisters: Reimagining the meaning of sisterhood.* New York, NY: Continuum.

Downing, C. (Ed.) (1991). *Mirrors of the self: Archetypal images that shape your life.* Los Angeles, CA: Jeremy P. Tarcher.

Downing, C. (1992). *Women's mysteries: Toward a poetics of gender.* New York, NY: Crossroads.

Downing, C. (1993). *Gods in our midst: Mythological images of the masculine: A woman's view.* New Orleans, LA: Spring Journal.

Easton, D., & Hardy, J. W. (2009). *The ethical slut: A practical guide to polyamory, open relationships, and other adventures.* New York, NY: Random House.

Edinger, E. (1972). *Ego and archetype.* Boston, MA: Shambhala.

Edinger, E. (1991). *Anatomy of the psyche: Alchemical symbolism in psychotherapy.* Chicago, IL: Open Court.

Engel, M. (2009). *Bear.* Toronto, Canada: McClelland & Stewart.

Estés, C. P. (1992). *Women who run with the wolves: Myths and stories of the wild woman archetype.* New York, NY: Random House.

Freud, S. (1933). *New introductory lectures on psycho-analysis.* New York, NY: Norton.

Gergen, K. J. (1985, March). The social constructionist movement in modern psychology. *American Psychologist, 40*(3), 266-275.

Gibran, K. (1923). *The prophet.* London, England: Wordsworth Editions.

Gilligan, C. (2002). *The birth of pleasure: A new map of love.* New York, NY: Random House.

Goodchild, V. (1997). *Eros and chaos: The sacred mysteries and dark shadows of love.* Lake Worth, FL: Nicolas-Hays.

Griffin, S. (1978). *Woman and nature: The roaring inside her.* San Francisco, CA: Sierra Club Books.

Harding, M. E. (1970). *The way of all women.* Boston, MA: Shambhala.

Harding, M. E. (1971). *Woman's mysteries: Ancient and modern.* Boston, MA: Shambhala.

Harris, B. (2007). *The fire and the rose: The wedding of spirituality and sexuality.* Wilmette, IL: Chiron.

Hartley, L. (2004). *Somatic psychology: Body, mind and meaning.* London, England: Whurr.

Hillman, J. (1972). *The myth of analysis.* New York, NY: Northwestern University Press.

Hillman, J. (1975). *Re-visioning psychology.* New York, NY: Harper & Row.

Hillman, J. (1989). *A blue fire.* New York, NY: Harper & Row.

Hillman, J. (2005). *Senex and puer* (G. Slater, Ed.). Putnam, CT: Spring.

Hillman, J. (2007a). *Aphrodite's justice.* Napoli, Italy: La Conchiglia.

Hillman, J. (2007b). *Mythic figures.* Putnam, CT: Spring.

Hillman, J., & Pozzo, L. (1983). Loving. In *Inter views: Conversations with Laura Pozzo on psychotherapy, biography, love, soul, dreams, work, imagination, and the state of the culture* (pp. 177-194). New York, NY: Harper & Row.

Hollis, J. (1998). *The Eden project: In search of the magical other.* Toronto, Canada: Inner City Books.

hooks, b. (2002). *Communion: The female search for love.* New York, NY: HarperCollins.

Johnson, R. A. (1983). *We: Understanding the psychology of romantic love.* New York, NY: HarperCollins.

Johnson, R. A. (1987). *Ecstasy: Understanding the psychology of joy.* New York, NY: HarperCollins.

Johnson, R. A. (1989). *She: Understanding feminine psychology.* New York, NY: HarperCollins.

Jung, C. G. (1961). *Memories, dreams, reflections.* New York, NY: Vintage Books.

Jung, C. G. (1968). *Man and his symbols.* London, England: Dell.

Jung, C. G. (1969). *Aion.* (R. F. C. Hull, Trans.). In H. Read et al. (Series Eds.), *The collected works of C. G. Jung* (Vol. 9ii, pp. 23-71). Princeton, NJ: Princeton University Press. (Original work published 1959)

Jung, C. G. (1969). The transcendent function. In R. F. C. Hull (Trans.), *The collected works of C. G. Jung* (Vol. 8, pp. 67-91). Princeton, NJ: Princeton University Press. (Original work published in 1929)

Jung, C. G. (1976). *The visions seminars* (Vol. 2). New York, NY: Spring.

Jung, C. G. (1997). Patterns of behavior and archetypes. In R. F. C. Hull (Trans.), *The collected works of C. G. Jung* (Vol. 8, pp. 200-217). Princeton, NJ: Princeton University Press. (Original work published 1937)

Jung, C. G. (2010). *Answer to Job.* Princeton, NJ: Princeton University Press. (Original work published 1958)

Kaparo, R. F. (2012). *Awakening somatic intelligence: The art and practice of embodied mindfulness.* Berkeley, CA: North Atlantic Books.

Kingma, D. R. (1998). *The future of love: The power of the soul in intimate relationships.* New York, NY: Doubleday.

Lao Tzu (1988). *Tao Te Ching* (S. Mitchell, Trans.). New York, NY: HarperCollins.

Le Grice, K. (2013a). *The personification of the opposites* (audio podcast). Retrieved from Pacifica Graduate Institute Course DJA 865 DesireToLearn site.

Le Grice, K. (2013b). *The stages of the conjunction* (audio podcast). Retrieved from Pacifica Graduate Institute Course DJA 865 DesireToLearn site.

Leonard, L. S. (1982). *The wounded woman: Healing the father–daughter relationship.* Boston, MA: Shambhala.

May, R. (1969). *Love and will.* New York, NY: Norton.

Mirdad, M. (2007). *Sacred sexuality: A manual for living bliss.* Bellingham, WA: Grail Press.

Moore, T. (1994). *Soul mates: Honoring the mysteries of love and relationship.* New York, NY: HarperCollins.

Moore, T. (1998). *The soul of sex: Cultivating life as an act of love.* New York, NY: HarperCollins.

Morin, J. (1995). *The erotic mind: Unlocking the inner sources of sexual passion and fulfillment.* New York, NY: HarperCollins.

Mozol, A. (2013). *Anima/animus* (audio podcast). Retrieved from Pacifica Graduate Institute Course DJA 840 DesireToLearn site.

Murdock, M. (1990). *The heroine's journey: Woman's quest for wholeness.* Boston, MA: Shambhala.

National Center for Health Statistics. (May 1991). *Monthly vital statistics report, 39*(12).

Neumann, E. (1956). *Amor and Psyche: The psychic development of the feminine.* New York, NY: Princeton University Press.

Oliver, M. (1983). *American primitive.* Boston, MA: Beacon Press.

Oliver, M. (1992). *New and selected poems.* Boston, MA: Back Bay Books.

Paris, G. (1986). *Pagan meditations: The worlds of Aphrodite, Artemis, and Hestia.* Putnam, CO: Spring.

Paris, G. (2008). How is psychology a mythology? In D. P. Slattery & G. Slater (Eds.), *Varieties of mythic experience* (pp. 211-229). Carpinteria, CA: Pacifica Graduate Institute Publications.

Perera, S. B. (1981). *Descent to the goddess: A way of initiation for women.* Toronto, Canada: Inner City Books.

Perluss, B. (2008). Climbing the alchemical mountain. *Psychological Perspectives, 51*(1), 87-107.

Perluss, E. (2013). *Psyche as nature* (audio podcast). Retrieved from Pacifica Graduate Institute Course DJA 860 DesireToLearn site.

Qualls-Corbett, N. (1988). *The sacred prostitute: Eternal aspect of the feminine.* Toronto, Canada: Inner City Books.

Raffa, J. B. (2012). *Healing the sacred divide: Making peace with ourselves, each other, and the world.* Burdett, NY: Larson.

Rilke, R. (1975). *Rilke on love and other difficulties.* New York, NY: Norton.

Romanyshyn, R. (2007). *The wounded researcher: Research with soul in mind.* New Orleans, LA: Spring Journal Books.

Roszak, T. (1992). *The voice of the earth: An exploration of eco-psychology.* Grand Rapids, MI: Phanes Press.

Rumi (1995). *The essential Rumi* (C. Barks, Trans.). New York, NY: HarperOne.

Rumi (2001). *The soul of Rumi: A new collection of ecstatic poems* (C. Barks, Trans.). New York, NY: HarperOne.

Sabini, M. (Ed.) (2008). *The earth has a soul: C. G. Jung on nature, technology & modern life.* Berkeley, CA: North Atlantic Books.

Sanford, J. (1980). *The invisible partners: How the male and female in each of us affects our relationships.* Mahwah, NJ: Paulist Press.

Sappho. (2002). *Poems and fragments* (S. Lombardo, Trans.). Indianapolis, IN: Hackett.

Schwartz-Salant, N. (1998). *The mystery of human relationship: Alchemy and the transformation of the self.* New York: NY: Routledge.

Shaw, M. (1994). *Passionate enlightenment: Women in Tantric Buddhism.* Princeton, NJ: Princeton University Press.

Slater, G. (2011). *The transcendent function* (audio podcast). Retrieved from Pacifica Graduate Institute Course DJA 720 DesireToLearn site.

Snyder, G. (1990). *The practice of the wild.* Berkeley, CA: Counterpoint.

Spiegelman, M., & Miyuki, M. (1985). *Buddhism and Jungian psychology.* Phoenix, AZ: Falcon Press.

Storr, A. (1983). *The essential Jung: Selected writings*. Princeton, NJ: Princeton University Press.

Tarnas, R. (1991). *The passion of the Western mind: Understanding the ideas that have shaped our world view*. New York, NY: Ballantine.

Tempest Williams, T. (1994). Undressing the bear. In *An unspoken hunger* (pp. 51-59). New York, NY: Pantheon.

Tolman, D. L., & Brydon-Miller, M. (2001). *From subjects to subjectivities: A handbook of interpretive and participatory methods*. New York, NY: New York University Press.

von Franz, M.-L. (1980a). *Alchemy: An introduction to the symbolism and the psychology*. Toronto, Canada: Inner City Books.

von Franz, M.-L. (1980b). *The psychological meaning of redemption motifs in fairytales*. Toronto, Canada: Inner City Books.

von Franz, M.-L. (1995). *Projection and re-collection in Jungian psychology: Reflections of the soul*. Chicago, IL: Open Court.

von Franz, M.-L. (1999). *The cat: A tale of feminine redemption*. Toronto, Canada: Inner City Books.

von Franz, M.-L. (2001). *Golden ass of Apuleius: The liberation of the feminine in man*. Boston, MA: Shambhala.

Whitmont, E. C. (1969). *The symbolic quest: Basic concepts of analytical psychology*. Princeton, NJ: Princeton University Press.

Whyte, D. (1990). *Where many rivers meet*. Langley, WA: Many Rivers Press.

Wikman, M. (2004). *The pregnant darkness: Alchemy and the rebirth of consciousness*. Berwick, ME: Nicolas-Hays.

Wilhelm, R. (1931). *The secret of the golden flower: A Chinese book of life*. San Diego, CA: Book Tree.

Woodman, M. (1982). *Addicted to perfection: The still unravished bride*. Toronto, Canada: Inner City Books.

Woodman, M. (1985). *The pregnant virgin: A process of psychological transformation*. Toronto, Canada: Inner City Books.

Woodman, M. (1990). *The ravaged bridegroom: Masculinity in women*. Toronto, Canada: Inner City Books.

Woodman, M. (1993). *Conscious femininity: Interviews with Marion Woodman*. Toronto, Canada: Inner City Books.

Yalom, I. D. (1989). *Love's executioner and other tales of psychotherapy*. New York, NY: HarperCollins.

CPSIA information can be obtained
at www.ICGtesting.com
Printed in the USA
BVHW061923230120
570306BV00005B/272